Faith, Family, Friends, Freedom

The Life and Legacy of Daisy Harris Wade

Anthony J. Harris

Tandem Light Press
950 Herrington Rd.
Suite C128
Lawrenceville, GA 30044
www.tandemlightpress.com

Copyright © 2015 by Anthony J. Harris

All rights reserved. No part of this book may be reproduced, scanned, or transmitted in any printed, electronic, mechanical, including photocopying, recording, or any information storage and retrieval system, without permission in writing from the publisher. Please do not participate in or encourage piracy of copyrighted materials in violation of the author's rights.

Tandem Light Press paperback edition June 2015

ISBN: 978-0-9861660-7-5
Library of Congress Control Number: 2015944183

PRINTED IN THE UNITED STATES OF AMERICA

Contents

Acknowledgments..V
Daisy's Family Tree..VII
Introduction...XV
Chapter 1: Faith..1
Chapter 2: Family...25
Chapter 3: Friends...75
Chapter 4: Freedom...89
Conclusion...107
Recipes...109
About the Author..113

ACKNOWLEDGMENTS

A year ago, Daisy asked me to write her biography. I believe she knew she was nearing the end of her life, and she wanted to tell her story. Her desire to tell her story was not for ego gratification. Rather, it was her way of passing on to current and future generations of friends and family a written narrative about the role that her faith, family, friends, and fight for freedom played in setting priorities in her life.

Having already written several books, I was anxious to add her biography to my list of publications. Regrettably, time did not allow me to complete the book before she passed away. Nonetheless, hers is a story that needs to be told, and it has been my great honor to tell it. I did not, however, tell it all by myself. Many others generously contributed to this homage to her.

First and foremost, I acknowledge Daisy Harris Wade for being a wonderful mother to three very grateful and blessed sons. I speak for myself and my brothers in saying that while she was alive and even in her death, she taught us how to love. She believed to her core what the Apostle Paul wrote to the Corinthians: *Three things will last forever – faith, hope, and love – and the greatest of these is love* (1 Corinthians 13:13).

Second, thanks to my brothers, James Jr. and Harold for their valuable contributions and memory joggers that helped unlock some wonderful and sometimes painful hidden memories. Beyond their contributions to this book, we share a bond that has existed since we were toddlers, thanks to two great parents.

I acknowledge the contributions of many friends and family members who submitted "Daisy Stories." A special thanks to my wife, Smitty, my son Michael, and my daughter, Ashley, for their unwavering support and encouragement. I want to give special recognition to Harold Harris, Jr.,

Daisy's grandson, who lived with her and cared for her throughout her illness. He was a godsend, and my brothers and I are forever grateful to him for being there for her. A few nights before Daisy passed away, Harold Jr. was at her bedside at 3:00 a.m. at the Windham House, holding her hand and playing her favorite gospel tunes on his telephone. That must have been a special moment for both of them. Although Daisy was not consciously aware of his presence, I am confident that spiritually, she was not only aware, but she was also smiling inside.

I also want to express appreciation to my sister-in-law, Lauraetta, Harold's wife, for her devotion to Daisy. Lauraetta often said she was blessed to have Daisy as another mother after her own mother passed away.

Finally, I acknowledge members of Daisy's family, whom she loved and adored, and who loved and adored her just as much. I have attempted to chart out a portion of her family tree to give the reader a snapshot of the family roots that produced her and the roots that she produced. Daisy loved her family. I know if she were overseeing this project, she would want to include everyone, alive and deceased, in this acknowledgement. I have endeavored to do so.

Daisy's Family Tree

Parents

Annie B. Griffin and Joe B. Griffin

Grandparents

Tiny (McAlpine) Dillard and Floyd McAlpine, Jr. (Annie B.'s Parents)
Reverend Elbert Griffin and Emma Smith Griffin (Joe B.'s Parents)

Great Grandparents

Horace Dillard and Martha Dillard (Annie B.'s Paternal Grandparents)
Floyd McAlpine, Sr. and Cinthia McAlpine (Annie B.'s Maternal Grandparents)

Aunts and Uncles

Martha Samuels
Eugene McAlpine
Kate McAlpine
Lucinda McAlpine
Lettie Ann Green

Minnie McAlpine
Rebecca McAlpine

Children

James Harris, Jr.
Anthony J. Harris
Harold E. Harris
Joann Harris (Stepdaughter)

Grandchildren

Kevin Harris, Sr. (Harold)
Dorian Harris (James)
Leslie Diggins (James)
Ashley Harris (Anthony)
Stephen Harris (Harold)
Stephon Harris (Harold)
Michael Harris (Anthony)
Jasmine Coicou (James)
Whitney Harris (Harold)
Antwan Harris (James)
Travon Sampson (James)
Angel Kia Vasser (James)
Harold Harris, Jr. (Harold)

Kenya Stinyard (James)

Great Grandchildren

Bianca Harris Core (Stephen)
Janiya Harris (Stephon)
Carter Harris Core (Stephen)
Jaeli Harris (Stephon)
Jace Harris (Stephon)
Trina Spencer (Kevin)
Kevin Harris, Jr. (Kevin)
Nila Harris (Stephen)
Chloe Ware (Stephen)
Ariana Harris (Dorian)
Christian Diggins (Leslie)
Taylor Diggins (Leslie)
Avery Lee Coicu (Jasmine)
Imani McNeil (Kia)
Jauda Lundy (Kia)
Javon Harris (Antwan)

Siblings

Elbert Griffin (Deceased)
Richard Oliver, Sr. (Deceased)

Floyd Oliver, Sr. (Deceased)
Emma Booth (Deceased)
Eugene Griffin (Deceased)
James Griffin (Deceased)
Joe Griffin, Jr. (Deceased)
Robert Lee Griffin (Deceased)
Joseph Griffin (Still born)
Louise Hayes
Angelia Griffin (Adopted Sister)

Sisters-in-Law and Brothers-in-Law

Dora Harris
Fannie (Tina) Griffin
Rolande Griffin (Deceased)
Yoshimi Oliver (Deceased)
Dorothy Jean Griffin
Johnnie Harris (Deceased)
Helen Harris (Deceased)
Ethyl Oliver (Deceased)
Luther Hayes
Joe Booth (Deceased)
Isaiah Thompson (Deceased)
Harold Harris (Deceased)
Herman Harris, Jr. (Deceased)

Leon Harris (Deceased)

Daughters-in-Law

Smithenia Harris
Lauraetta Harris
Kay Fields
Tracey Harris

Nieces and Nephews

Barbara (Barb) McKinley
Beverly Jones
Patricia Griffin
Dorothy Annette Griffin
Jeanette Griffin
Joe Curtis Griffin (Deceased)
Tangelia Thompson
Joseph Rodney Booth
Maury Eugene Booth (Deceased)
Floyd Oliver, Jr.
Miyoko Minor
Shizua Oliver
Jacqueline McCoy (Deceased)
Linda Oliver (Deceased)

Bernice (Bonnie) Oliver

Richard (Ricky) Oliver

Elaine Maxwell

R. Laverne Rice

Yolanda Lacey

Regina Mims

Belinda Heath

Simone White

Monika Nicholson

Elbert Griffin

Deborah Holmes

Jeannie Anderson

Terry Farrell

Sharon Jenkins

Debbie Cheatham

Carol Harris

Bruce Harris

Leon (June Bug) Harris, Jr.

Tracy Lynn Harris

Charlene Harris

Helen Harris

Cousins

Eloise Huddleston

James Anderson

Fred Anderson

Elizabeth Green

Willie James Green

Jim Green

Bessie Lee Boykins

Introduction

Daisy Lee Griffin Harris Wade was born Daisy Lee Griffin, one of ten children (and the oldest of three girls) of Joe B. and Annie B. Griffin, in racially segregated Hattiesburg, Mississippi, on April 22, 1931, two years after the start of the Great Depression. She died October 29, 2014 in slightly less segregated Hattiesburg, Mississippi, exactly 85 years after the start of the Great Depression. Although the certificate of her birth marked the beginning of her life and the certificate of her death marked the end of it, the life that she lived between birth and death transcends both a birth and a death certificate.

Since the beginning of time, the cycle of birth, living, and death has been the ultimate human equalizer, granting succor or favor to no one. Without exception, all humans, no matter their race, gender, or income cycle through those three stages of being. Essentially, we are born; we live; then we die. What, then, distinguishes one life from another, given that all humans experience the same cycle of life—birth, living, and death? What makes a person's life—that differentiating period between birth and death—meaningful, memorable, and worthy of honor and reverence? In the case of Daisy Lee Griffin Harris Wade, that answer is simple yet profound. What distinguishes her living and gives her a well-earned place of honor in the hearts and minds of those who loved her was an untiring devotion to her *Faith, Family, Freedom, and Friends.*

What follows is not only a tribute to her, but a reflection on a well-lived life that has served and will continue to serve as an inspiration to others. In reading this book, someone will find encouragement, inspiration, and hope. One of her humble wishes was that someone's life would be changed for the better because of something she said or did.

The book also contains "Daisy Stories" written by friends and family members. Their stories, printed in italics, are testaments to the strength of their relationships and the impact that she had on their lives.

There are several of Daisy recipes, including her famous banana pudding. Although the recipe for that renowned banana pudding of hers is included, do not be surprised if yours does not taste quite the same as hers. My brother, Junior and I both tried making it per her instructions and ingredients. Junior's experience with making her banana pudding was exactly as mine. After biting into it, I tasted a delicious piece of pudding. It was definitely mouth watering, but it was not exactly like Daisy's. I called her and reported to her that I was pleased with the pudding, but it did not taste as good as hers. She chuckled, and said, "I might have left a little something out—that is my secret." If you try her recipe, please let me know how it turns out.

And no story about Daisy's life would be complete without pictures. She loved collecting pictures of family members and friends and sharing them. Some of the pictures are black and white and others are in color. Either way, she felt pictures were vital visual narratives that revealed more than the printed or spoken word. And behind every picture was a fascinating story about her *Faith, Family, Friends, and Freedom*, which made her beam with joy when recounting.

***

No doubt, many lives have already been changed from simply knowing her, listening to her, and loving her. The reader of this book will learn about Daisy, about her joys, disappointments, and dreams; about her hopes, achievements, and recognitions; about her grit, raw courage, and magnetic personality; and about her foibles, imperfections, and humanness. Once the reader gets to know Daisy, they will find something about her that is worthy of emulation. That would bring a big smile to her face as she looks down from among that great cloud of witnesses who have gone home to join the Father.

Throughout the book, I use my mom's first name—Daisy—instead of mother, mama, or mom. In fact, since my brothers and I were able to talk, we called her Daisy. And our use of her first name was not a sign of disrespect. When my brothers and I were infants and toddlers, along with our parents, we lived with my grandparents—Daisy's parents. As we learned to identify family members by name, we naturally used the names that everyone else used. Everyone called our mom Daisy, and so did we. They called my dad, Woofie, and so did we. We did the same for my grandmother, whom everyone called Mama and our grandfather was called Daddy. As we grew older, Daisy and Woofie were satisfied with our using their first names; and according to Daisy, she and Woofie only briefly insisted that we call them Mama and Daddy. However, since we had become so accustomed to using their first names, we never got into the habit of using any other names. Our friends and other similar-age relatives, however, did not have such a privilege. They had to use a title before her name, such as Aunt Daisy, Grandma Daisy, or Miss Daisy.

***

I miss Daisy very much. And the hurt that I feel everyday seems like it will never go away. There are competing images of her constantly coursing through my mind. One set of images is of her as a healthy, energetic woman. She is smiling, laughing, talking, singing, cradling a child in her arms, sewing, or preparing a meal. The other is of her lying in bed in a very fragile state. She is weeping, disoriented, frail, weak, tired, sleeping, or speaking inaudibly. I have learned to welcome both sets of images and allow them to find a place in my head and heart. I have come to realize that both sets of images represent the existential reality of who Daisy was—healthy and fragile.

Despite missing her so much, I am comforted in the Word. I am especially comforted by these words, found in Revelation 14:13—*Then I heard a voice from heaven say, "Write: Blessed are the dead who die in the Lord from now on. Yes, says the Spirit, they will rest from their labor, for their deeds will follow them."* Surely, my dear, sweet Daisy died in the Lord; and in doing so, He has given her raptured soul rest, just beyond the river. Her good deeds not only followed her on to Heaven, but they remain on this side as markers of a well-lived life. The sweet sorrow of her passing causes me to miss her physical presence, but I also feel her love and spirit warmly wrapped around me every single day.

I am also comforted in these words from 2 Timothy 4:7, which so aptly sum up her life and death: *You fought the good fight. You finished the race. You kept the faith.* And I can imagine that upon receiving her in Heaven, the Lord held her tightly to His bosom and whispered, *Welcome home, my good and faithful servant. Now take your rest.*

Chapter 1
Faith

Nothing was more important to Daisy than her faith. For sure, her family, friends, and freedom mattered greatly to her, but first and foremost in her life was her relationship with God. Before she was a mother to my brothers and me... before she was a wife to Woofie... before she was a daughter to Annie B. and Joe B.... before she was a sister to her siblings... before she was a friend to so many... and before she became a loyal foot soldier in the struggle for civil rights... she was first a child of God. She took to heart that sacred and holy relationship she had with God and arranged priorities in her life accordingly. She grasped the wisdom of Matthew in 10:37 — *Whoever loves father or mother more than me is not worthy of me,* and whoever loves son or daughter more than me is not worthy of me. She was clear about how she should live her life, and she was gifted in discerning what was relevant to her salvation and what was mere living in the flesh. She enjoyed life, but never took it for granted. She was grounded in her faith, believing that *faith is the substance of things hoped for, the evidence of things not seen* (Hebrew 11:1).

In living out her faith, she sought to be holy, not haughty; to be humbled, not proud; and to be forgiving, not vindictive. Not one to brag about her religious fervor, she allowed her faith to speak for itself. She abided in the wisdom of the Apostle James (2:17), who wrote, Faith without works is dead.

Her faith was at work, for example, whenever she offered words of condolence and sympathy to someone mourning the loss of a loved one. Often, her expressions of sympathy were in the form of a carefully selected card, a phone call, a visit, or one of her famous banana puddings. Daisy was affectionately known among black funeral directors in Hattiesburg as *The Inspector*. Because she attended so many funerals, they sought out her opinion regarding how well the deceased were presented or how well the staff performed their duties. In every case, she knew the deceased and often spoke passionately about that person during the Words from Friends portion of the service. My brothers and I received comments from many friends following her home-going service expressing their admiration of how well the service was conducted. I replied, "The Inspector would have approved and been proud."

***

If Daisy had only two nickels and someone else had none, she would cheerfully sacrifice one of her nickels; and if one nickel was not enough, she would gladly sacrifice the other. She routinely sent birthday cards to her grandchildren, often with two or three dollars tucked inside. It was not much money, but the intent was to add a little extra to a simple but heart-felt expression of love and in her words, "to keep the haints off of you." Very likely, she could have found some other use for those dollar bills, but in her heart she was bringing a smile to someone's face.

Through a conversation with a young mother who was a member of her church, Daisy learned that the young, single mother was struggling financially and was having difficulty clothing herself and her children. The next day, Daisy bundled several boxes of children's and women's clothes, and without fanfare gave them to the young mother who expressed her thanks with a big hug punctuated with uncontrollable tears of joy. She performed those acts of faith without prompting, solicitation, or boastfulness. Rather, she performed those and countless other acts of mercy and love because she believed her faith required her to do so. To not do those things, she believed, was to be un-Christ-like and to be unfaithful.

On many occasions, Daisy would send care packages to my brothers and me, although we were grown and married. Those carefully wrapped packages generally consisted of such items as sweaters, belts, socks, coats, and underwear, which she purchased at one of her favorite stores—Hudson's or Dirt Cheap. Sometimes the packages also included various and sundry items for our kids and wives. I knew three things about those packages. One, she likely sacrificed something she needed or wanted in order to purchase those items. Two, while we did not necessarily need those items, it was about the gift giver more than about the gifts themselves. And most importantly, it was about an expression of love from a mother and grandmother to her children and grands.

When I was in my senior year of college in 1974, I was invited to participate in a study abroad program in Bogota, Colombia. The program required a $700 deposit, most of which I did not have. As a Spanish major at the University of Southern Mississippi, I was excited about the opportunity to live in Colombia for two months with a non-English speaking family, improving my Spanish-speaking skills and immersing myself in another culture. I recall sitting with Daisy one morning in the kitchen eating some of her delicious grits, bacon, and eggs. She could tell from the look on my face that I was bothered by something. "Ant, everything okay? Seems like something's troubling you, son," she said.

"I was invited to go on this study abroad program to South America— Bogota, Colombia. I have to pay a big deposit by next week or I won't be able to go," I said. With my fork, I placed a serving of grits, eggs, and crumbled bacon, all mixed together, into my mouth.

"How much is the deposit?" she asked. "It's a lot. I might be able to come up with it if I get some extra hours at work. But by the time I get paid, the deadline will be passed," I said.

"How much is it?" she asked.

"Daisy, it's too much. It's seven hundred dollars," I said.

She let out a moan, stood up from the table, and placed her dishes in the sink. "Son, don't worry. The Lord will make a way somehow. He always does," she said.

I finished the last fork full of my mixture of grits, eggs, and bacon, put the dishes in the sink, and told her I had to leave for class. A few days later, as we were having breakfast—more grits, bacon, and eggs stirred and mixed together—she excused herself and went to her bedroom. After several minutes, she returned with a white, sealed envelope. "Ant, here, take this. It's for you," she said, sliding the envelope underneath my left hand.

"What's this, Daisy?" I asked. "Just open it and you will see," she said. I opened it and looked inside, and there were seven one-hundred dollar bills. "Oh, Daisy, where did you get this? And what is it for?" I asked.

"Don't worry about where it came from, and it is for your deposit so you can go on that trip to wherever you said," she said.

"Bogota, Colombia," I said.

"That's right. Now you take this money and give it to whoever you suppose to give it to. It ain't too late is it?" she asked.

"No, Daisy. It's not too late. But you didn't have to do this. You have your own bills, and you don't need to be spending your money on me."

"Look, son. I wanted to do this. You are my son, and I know this trip is important to you. You don't ever know when another chance to go to another country is gonna come along. So, you just take this money and go and give it to whoever supposed to get it out there at that college. Now that's all I got to say about it. I'm getting ready to go to work. I will see you later on this evening," she said.

"Thanks, Daisy. I guess when you said the Lord's going to make a way, you knew what you were talking about, didn't you?" I asked.

"He ain't failed me yet," she said as she disappeared down the hallway to her bedroom. Once again, she had come to my rescue and became the answer to my prayer. Although she told me not to worry about how she got the money, I did. I worried because I was sure she borrowed it from one of the loan companies that she and Woofie had used many times. But that was who she was. She was putting her faith to work, and in her own special way she was responding to a quote from Dr. King: *Life's most urgent question is: What are you doing for others?*

***

Whitney Earl Harris, Grandson

When I was around the age of 10, I can remember spending a holiday with my brother Junior and my cousin Jasmine at Grandma Daisy's home, as we had done many times before. Each time we were together, Grandma always made sure to take us everywhere she went. We would visit a lot of the sick members of her church, nursing homes and hospitals. This one particular weekend we had been in and out the house all day, and it was starting to get late. When we got home it had to be around 8pm. Later that night SHE MADE A PHONE CALL to somebody, and woke us up to go with her. Of course we were mad! She got up and made two to-go boxes of food. It had to be around 11 o'clock at night. When we were younger, the neighborhood was not that safe to be out that night. We ended up in a bad neighborhood with drug dealers and all kinds of people outside. Here the four of us are in this white car, it's dark, and folks are watching us. Grandma tells us to stay in the car and not to open the door for anyone. She then goes to this run down pitch black house and disappears. We're looking at each other like "Really Grandma?"

Junior says, "Man we should have gone in there with her."

But we were scared to leave the car at this point. So after about ten minutes, she comes back to the car. All of us were mad at this point, and I say, "Why would you do this? This couldn't wait till the morning? It wasn't safe for you to go out there alone."

Junior said, "Right! You got all these crack heads out here, and you don't know what they are gonna do with that food. They may sell it or trade it for more drugs."

Now Grandma is mad at this point; she stops the car, looks back at Junior and says, "Shut your ass up now!"

We look at each other like, did she really cuss at us? She said, "I don't want to hear that talk. I called them to check on them. Just because they have a bad habit doesn't mean we stop caring for them. We're supposed to keep loving no matter what!" Now that made us all stop and think. We felt so bad and were quiet the rest of the trip home.

So I try my best now more than ever to show that love. No matter how people have wronged me, or I have wronged them in the past, I must love them, even if they don't ask for forgiveness. Grandma is on my mind more than ever and I'm grateful she has shown me how to love.

***

Daisy's faith journey began at the age of 15, when she joined Starlight Missionary Baptist Church, a small, white cinder block building located at 1413 Gravel Line Road in Hattiesburg. A tiny building with a big heart, Starlight was the church family for Daisy and her three sons for decades. Located within spitting distance of a railroad track, the congregation and choir were not deterred when competing with the roar of a slow-moving freight train and its blaring horn while listening to the preacher's message or searching for the right pitch for a song. The love flowing from that church was as big as its physical size was small. It was populated by some devout, God-loving people, who helped shaped the spiritual lives of Daisy and her three boys. Memories from my childhood flood my mind when I recall the faces and voices of the precious people with whom we worshiped at that little white church on the gravel line—Mrs. Ford, Mr. Murphy, Judy Murphy, Shirley Murphy, Elbert Murphy, Harold (Peanut) Murphy, Joann Murphy, Sara Murphy, Mrs. Lucille Floyd, Mr. and

Mrs. Rucker, Bernice Rucker, Junior Rucker, L.C. Rucker, Ray Rucker, Lora Lee Rucker, Jessie Mae, Willie Louis, Floyd Rucker, Gladys Rucker, Dot Rucker, Mrs. Sims, Mr. and Mrs. Barnes, Miss Olivia Stewart, Mrs. Evelyn Stewart, Mrs. Tillman, Mrs. Mamie Roebuck, Mrs. Willie Adams, Georgia (Sallye) Hammond, Mrs. Mae Nelson, Virginia Nelson, Robert Newton, Sammie Newton, Gwen Newton, Derrell Newton, Elaine Newton, Elizabeth Patterson, Ernest Whitlock, Mrs. Lillie Gaddis, Earlene Gaddis, Gerlene Gaddis, Mr. and Mrs. Coleman, Mr. Cal, Mr. and Mrs. Washington.

Starlight was a haven for Daisy and a welcoming place where she gladly offered her gifts, talents, and presence. Having already become an accomplished pianist by age 15, under the tutelage of Mrs. Callie Mae Walker and Mrs. Olivia Hudson, she accepted her calling to take on the duties of directing and providing piano accompaniment for both the Senior and Junior choirs at Starlight. She maintained those duties well into her 70s. I have many vivid memories of Daisy rehearsing the choirs for both special and routine occasions, such as Pastoral Day, Easter programs, Christmas programs, and the 1st and 2nd Sunday Singing Unions.

In those early days when I was a child, Pastoral Day was generally the fourth Sunday of the month, when the Reverend J.J. Jones conducted regular worship service at Starlight. The other three Sundays, church service consisted mainly of Sunday School. It was very common in those days for many black pastors to be simultaneously employed by several churches and to preach at a different church each Sunday. Starlight was generally fourth in that rotation for Reverend Jones, thus Pastoral Day at Starlight was the fourth Sunday of each month. I learned later that one of the reasons that many black preachers took on several churches was, in part, to earn a living. Reverend Jones could not take care of his family on the salary he earned at a single church. No doubt, earning a salary at three other churches helped only slightly. So, he painted houses to supplement the income he earned from being a pastor at four different churches.

***

Johnny Jones, Member of Starlight Missionary Baptist Church

I first met Miss Daisy when I went to Vacation Bible School at Starlight as a little kid. I did not always want to go Bible School, but since my dad, Reverend J.J. Jones was the pastor, I was expected to be there. But the reason I really wanted to go was because Miss Daisy was the teacher for the class I was in. From the time I was a child to becoming an adult, Miss Daisy has had a big impact on my life.

She inspired me in so many ways. I was talking with her one day at church about things in my life that I wasn't proud of. I wondered if someone who was a sinner like me could still be saved. She told me three things that set my heart and soul to rest. First, she said everybody has done things they are not proud of. We are all sinners and that no matter what we have done, God will forgive us.

Second, she said it's what's on the inside that really counts. In other words, what's in my heart and my relationship with the Lord was what was going to give me salvation. Three, she said that whatever I had done was between me and the Lord and that I would have to walk through it and pray for wisdom. A light bulb came on because of what she said to me. I was able to accept the fact that, despite my sins, all I had to do was to repent and ask for God's forgiveness.

When I recommitted my life to Christ a few years ago at Starlight, I think she was crying harder than I was. She not only cried, but she prayed for me. Her prayers and tears seemed like they put God's spirit right in me and made me know that God had a purpose and plan for my life.

Miss Daisy crosses my mind every day. Whenever I pass her house, I still expect to see her white car parked in the driveway. She has been a blessing to me, and I will miss her so much. After I lost my mother a long time ago, I always kept a picture in my heart of her smiling. That really helped me to get through the grief and pain. Now that Miss Daisy has passed away, I keep a picture in my heart of her smiling. It helps, but it still hurts to know that she won't be here anymore. But I know she is in heaven, and I just hope and pray that the Lord will see fit to let me see her again.

***

I have memories, as a young boy in my adolescent and pre-teen days, of Pastoral Day. One of those memories was the fact that church service was to begin at 11:00 a.m., at least according to the Program of Worship. (Another monthly feature of the Program of Worship was an insert that contained the names of each church member and how much they had tithed so far that year. Talk about holding people accountable!) But rarely did service begin at that time. Instead, it started right around noon and lasted well past 2:00 p.m. Reverend Jones said that he preached by the spirit and not by the clock, although there was a clock hanging on the wall opposite the pulpit, in his direct line of vision. With the following order of worship, it is easy to understand why church seemed to last as long as it did. Of course, as a child, I started feeling a bit restless after the first 30 minutes, but dared not let Daisy see me acting restlessly. And sitting in wooden pews that offered no cushion for my rear end, it was sometimes hard for me to avoid the inevitable restlessness.

Service began when the deacons decided it was time, usually around noon. Deacon Murphy and Deacon Rucker sat in chairs facing the congregation and led us in an opening devotional song, which they chanted, in the hymn lining tradition. After about fifteen minutes of the a capella devotional chant, one of the deacons would kneel on one knee with head bowed in front of one of the straw bottom, wooden, ladder back chairs and offer up a long, powerful prayer as the congregation moaned, hummed, and continued chanting in the hymn lining tradition. As soon as the deacon intoned a hearty "Amen," the other deacon would lead the congregation in a song, probably *Lord, Hold My Hand While I Run This Race*. The final stanza ended, and on cue from Daisy, the senior choir marched, in rhythm, into the sanctuary singing an introductory number, probably, *Hold to His Hand*. Once in the choir stand, the choir sang a Selection A and a Selection B, probably *Walk With Me and I Know the Lord Will Make A Way*.

Next, it was time for the offertory. Probably singing *We've Come this Far by Faith*, the congregation marched around the sanctuary and deposited their tithes and offerings into the straw-woven collection basket setting atop the mustard colored communion table that had the words, **In Remembrance of Me** inscribed on the front panel of the table. One of the deacons would send up a prayer of thanks for the offerings, no matter the size, he said. *Bless the gift and the giver that they may be used to glorify the Kingdom of the Lord.* After they gathered the tithes and offerings from the collection basket, the deacons retired to a room in the back of the church to count and secure the money.

Daisy would then begin to play a familiar tune on the old, brown, upright piano. That was the cue for the congregation to stand, young and old, and sing *Amazing Grace*. At the end of the final stanza, one of the deacons would motion to the ushers to come forward to retrieve their collection baskets for the benevolent offering. This time the ushers passed the basket among the congregation instead of everyone having to march around the sanctuary. It was sometimes a little humorous to see someone put a quarter in the basket and take out two dimes or make change for a one-dollar bill.

After the benevolent offering, Reverend Jones would stroll to the pulpit, read a passage from the Bible, offer a prayer, and then deliver a stirring message that went about 30-45 minutes. I knew it was stirring because, toward the end of the message, Mrs. Ford began to shout and run up and down the aisle, filled with the Holy Spirit. At the close of the message, Daisy would begin playing another familiar tune. The congregation would stand again and sing another congregational song, probably *Precious Lord, Take My Hand*. On the final stanza, Reverend Jones would announce that the doors of the church were open.

"Will there be one?" he asked several times.

The deacons would place a couple of chairs on either side of the communion table for anyone coming forward. If there was not one who was ready to transfer membership or become a candidate for baptism, Reverend Jones would wind up the service with a benediction; and the service officially ended with the congregation standing and singing *Blest*

Be the Ties that Bind. With a quick glance at the clock, I knew I was ready to go home, but not until Daisy said it was time to go. Church members lingered about, hugging, shaking hands, and saying their good-byes. It was what families did.

And if there was eating on the grounds, we would stay even longer. My brothers and I, along with other children and adults were responsible for helping set up the meals by setting out the vegetables, meats, breads, and desserts. After making sure there were enough seats, plates, silverware, drinks, and napkins for everyone, Reverend Jones blessed the food, and the eating and fellowshipping commenced. After the last morsel of food was eaten, dishes washed, tables cleaned, floor swept and the final bag of trash collected and discarded, only then was it time to go home.

Another memory of my early years as a member of Starlight was when once a year, Starlight would hold a week-long revival. Revival was an important time in the life of Starlight. It was an opportunity for members to revive their spirits and reconnect with and recommit to their spiritual journey. It was also a time to put the spotlight on Starlight. As a small church, Starlight relished the idea of having black people from all of Hattiesburg come to its place of worship and experience the overflowing love that oozed from that church.

For seven consecutive nights, usually in the fall, Starlight hosted its annual revival, and in doing so became the center of attention in the Hattiesburg black church community. Each night, the revival service was much like any other regular Pastoral Day service, with a couple of noticeable differences. One difference was that each night, a different church choir provided the musical selections, although Starlight's choir was on standby in case the invited choir did not show up. Choirs from other churches generally showed up when invited, in part, because of reciprocity. At some point, every black church in Hattiesburg would ask and be asked to provide the musical portion of revival. So, no church wanted to be a no-show when invited to sing at a revival. And also because this was a rare occasion to sing before a different congregation, the guest choir typically sang with extra energy and spirit.

Another difference was that, although there was a different choir each night, the same preacher delivered the sermon for the entire week. When it was time for the message, Reverend Jones made a few remarks, and then introduced the guest preacher. Reverend Hopkins, from Chicago, Illinois, was the guest preacher for every Starlight church revival that I can recall during my childhood. I surmised later, that Reverend Jones and Reverend Hopkins must have had an arrangement in which they served as the guest preacher at each church's revival service. At the end of each service, Reverend Hopkins, Reverend Jones and their families would dine at the home of one of the church members.

One particularly unforgettable evening occurred at our home when our entire family, including Woofie, and the Hopkins and Jones families dined at our home following an evening of revival worship. Hal's recollection of the events of that evening is included here. Everyone seemed to enjoy the fellowship time and Daisy's scrumptious entrée, despite the lack of conversation from Woofie, who was not a regular church-goer at the time and did not feel comfortable in the presence of two men of the cloth. For most of the evening, he ate his food and kept quiet. That is until Daisy served dessert, which was a homemade pound cake. She sliced the cake and first served the guests, then Woofie, and finally herself and my brothers and me. Reverend Hopkins was the first to offer his opinion of the cake.

"Sister Harris, you outdid yourself with this meal. And this cake is especially tasty," said Reverend Hopkins.

That opinion of Daisy's pound cake did not jibe with Woofie's, and after an hour of near total silence, he finally offered an opinion on the subject at hand. "That's a damn lie. This cake tastes like bubble gum. You just keep chewin', chewin', and chewin'," Woofie said as he rose from the table, tramped to his bedroom and slammed the door.

A naturally awkward and embarrassing moment brought the evening's meal and fellowship to an abrupt end. Reverend Hopkins, Reverend Jones and their families gathered themselves and exited the house, each offering Daisy a "God bless you, sister Harris..." Hal said that event affected him so much that he vowed that night that he would never eat cake again. And he has kept that vow, having never tasted any type of cake in fifty plus years.

Woofie also influenced our diet and choice of foods in other ways, but not as rudely as he had done with the pound cake incident. He maintained a strong dislike for the taste of cheese and butter, which apparently started in his childhood. One day, Daisy was serving grits and there was butter on the table. She liked butter, so she put it in her grits and on her toast. When she attempted to put butter on our grits and toast, he told my brothers and me not to eat butter or cheese because they were nasty. I believed him, and for decades, until I became an adult, I refused to eat cheese, only because Woofie had ingrained in me that the taste of cheese was terrible. His views about the unpleasantness of butter, however, did not affect me. I welcomed the taste of butter on my grits and toast and never ate either without a serving of butter.

***

Robert E. Harris, Member of Starlight Missionary Baptist Church

I first met Daisy when I was 13 years old, after I had moved to Hattiesburg from Shivers, Mississippi. She lived on Geneva Street, just around the corner from Starlight Baptist Church. One day I was passing her house, going to Mr. Gil's Grocery Store, and she was sitting on the front porch. She spoke, and I said hello. She asked me, "Do you belong to a church?"
I said, "No, I don't."

She asked me if I would consider joining Starlight Missionary Baptist Church. I knew about Starlight, but no one had ever asked me about joining. I told her, "Yes. I will consider joining." After I joined Starlight, we spent a lot of

time talking about Starlight, and she never forgot me. She always made me feel welcomed at church.

At age 24, I moved to California and stayed there for the next 40 years. I moved back to Hattiesburg in 2003, and one of the first people I saw was Daisy. First thing she said to me was, "Robert, you need to renew your membership at Starlight. I know you've been gone a long time, but Starlight is still your home church." I took her suggestion and recommitted my life to Christ and to Starlight and renewed my membership. Joining Starlight when I was a teenager and renewing my membership when I moved back were two of the best decisions I ever made in my life.

Many times, members of Starlight visited other churches, and Daisy would often drive us to those churches. I remember feeling so welcomed with the group because of what Daisy did. On those occasions and on others, she extended herself to make sure I was comfortable. She always encouraged and motivated me. I needed that and I thank her so much for being there to help me fit back in to the Starlight church family.

There was one occasion that I remember when I did the driving. It was when her sister was in the car wreck on the Coast. She was in really bad shape, and Starlight prayed for her healing. I drove Daisy and several members of the church to the Coast to visit her sister and pray for her recovery. It was a bittersweet trip, I recall. We were on a mission of healing for someone who was severely injured in a car wreck. And not just anyone, but the sister of our church sister, Daisy. But the trip to the Coast was also a lot of fun. We lightened the mood a little bit by talking, laughing, and having a really good time. I think she needed that. And so did the rest of us.

Daisy kept me informed about what was going on in the country and around the world. I would receive a phone call from her and she would ask if I was watching CNN. If I wasn't, she would tell me to quickly turn to that channel to watch something she thought I should know about. Without her phone calls, I am sure I would have missed out on lot of the news that was happening.

I am so happy she came into my life and made such a difference in it. There will never be anyone like her again. She was an icon at Starlight and in Hattiesburg. I am so grateful that she inspired my wife, Marilyn, and me in ways that we never would have imagined. The way she helped other people and sacrificed for them was something I will never forget. And I just pray that I can be half as inspiring to others as she was to me. I know that she is in heaven, and I am looking forward to seeing her up there one day. May she rest in peace and may God bless her.

***

Daisy was what most people today would call an old-school mother, especially when it came to instilling in my brothers and me the importance of church attendance. Unlike many parents today, she never once asked us whether or not we wanted to go to church. She never negotiated, pleaded, or begged us to go to Sunday School, church services, choir rehearsals, BTU (Baptist Training Union), singing unions, or to participate in Easter and Christmas programs. There were no nurseries to which babies and toddlers were sent. Crying babies were held and fanned by a parent or one of the ushers until they stopped crying. Daisy and the other adults in the church made sure we older children did not talk, chew gum, or engage in horseplay while church was going on. If a child forgot the rules of proper church etiquette, a swift whack on the bottom or a stern look quickly corrected that misbehavior.

Little did we know at the time, those loving men and women were instilling discipline in us and setting expectations about proper behavior such as respecting elders, respecting the speaker, sitting still and paying attention. Of course, when nature called and a trip to the restroom was absolutely necessary, it was common courtesy to show respect to the speaker or singers by holding up an index finger and as quietly and as inconspicuously as possible exit the sanctuary. The routine was the same when returning to the sanctuary.

Even more, when she attended one of the several other churches where she was the choir pianist, there were never any questions as to whether or not my brothers and I would also attend. She had one statement about church attendance: "You'd better be in that car when I crank it up!" Without fail, when that car started up, we were in the car, settled in our seats, decked out in our Sunday suits. Yes, even as children, my brothers and I wore suits that matched in both color and style because Daisy was also "old school" in her belief that whenever we went to church we should show proper respect by wearing our Sunday best.

The only reason we did not go to church was for genuine sickness, like stay-in-bed-running-a-fever sickness. She did not permit excuses such as, *I'm too tired. Church is boring.* Or, I just don't feel like going to church today. No purpose would be served by offering up one of those excuses, even if we truly felt that way. If we dared utter one of them, she would quickly retort, "I don't care how you feel. You're gonna feel something else if you are not in that car when I crank it up!"

Message clearly sent and clearly received.

Even if physically getting to church presented a challenge, she did not accept that as an excuse for not attending. For example, at one time, Woofie owned a small beige-colored car — the British-manufactured Hillman Husky Wagon that he purchased on credit through the Hercules Credit Union. The designer and manufacturer of the Hillman Husky Wagon did not intend for it to be a family vehicle, let alone one for a family of five. It came equipped with a standard transmission, two doors with a hatchback door, two small front bucket seats, and a back seat that could accommodate no more than two small children. Daisy had absolutely no idea how to drive a car with a manual transmission. Woofie, being the non-church-goer, was of no help. He never offered to drive us to church, and he lacked the patience to teach Daisy how to drive a stick shift. But did she let that keep us from going to church? You guessed it. No!

One Sunday morning, she announced, "Boys, it's 9:00, and we are leaving at 9:45. You'd better be in that car by the time I crank it up."

My brothers heard the announcement of the usual departure time, but we were not sure about how she was going to manage to get us from one side of town to the other, especially in a car she didn't know how to drive. At exactly 9:45, she exited the front door of the house with her three stair-step boys in tow. "Junior, you get up front, and Ant, you and Hal, get in the back," she commanded.

Junior grinned and licked out his tongue at Hal and me. "I'm riding shotgun, and y'all sitting in the back," he sang. He was feeling special that he got to ride shotgun without having to argue with Hal and me about who called it first.

"Stop teasing them boys, Junior, and turn around in that seat. Now, do you know how to shift these gears on this car? As much as you ride up here with your daddy, you must know something, more than I do," she said.

"Yeah, I watch Woofie all the time when he shifts the gears and he lets me do it sometimes," answered 13 year-old Junior. He had observed my father shifting gears and easily committed to memory the entire sequence and timing of each shift of the gears.

"Good. I thought so. I tried to learn it, but your daddy is so impatient. I just ain't had a chance to learn it. So, here's what you and me gonna do. I know I have to push the clutch in before the stick can be moved. So, I'm gonna push the clutch and you are gonna moved the stick to the right gear. You just have to tell when to push the clutch. You understand what we gonna do?" she asked.

"For real, Daisy. You gonna let me shift?" asked a grinning Junior as he looked back at Hal and me and showed more of his big beaver teeth.

"Yeah, boy. We can do this. Turn back around and leave them boys alone. Okay, let's go. We got to get Sunday School on time," she said.

"Okay, Daisy. Before you crank it up, you got to push the clutch in and hold it 'til I put it in gear. And don't forget to put your foot on the brake. Now, go ahead and turn the key," Junior instructed. The car responded with the familiar whine that announced the successful ignition of the engine.

"Alright, now that it's running, what do we do next?" asked Daisy.

"Hold on. Keep your foot on the clutch and brake and let me put it in reverse," Junior said as he effortlessly found the reverse position for the gift shift.

"Alright, now what?" she asked. "Let up off the brake and take your foot off the clutch," he answered. She followed his instructions, and slowly and jerkily, the car backed out of the driveway onto Fredna Avenue, and just as slowly and jerkily turned on Dabbs Street; then to Ronie Street; on to Front Street; left turn on to Main Street; right turn onto Highway 11 Bypass; and left to 1413 Gravel Line Road. And amazingly, in tandem, she and James drove that car from one side of town to another, each doing their part, alternately pressing the clutch and moving the stick to the correct position. Their timing was not always the best, which sometimes caused that unpleasant metal-on-metal sound that comes from of a gear being shifted without the clutch being fully engaged. But the Lord must have been watching over us, because we made it to church and back home in one piece.

On each trip to and from church that did not involve tandem driving, Daisy would noticeably slow down as she entered the curve on Market Street. Of course, that was because it was a curve, and thus, required a decrease in speed in order to maintain control of the vehicle. But there could also be another reason for decelerating. Either of the two reasons for slowing down triggered a predictable Pavlovian response from my brothers and me—either smiles or frowns. If she slowed down only because of the curve in the street, we frowned. If, however, she slowed down and pulled into a parking space in front of the donut shop on

Market Street, we smiled. In fact, we would do a happy dance and bounce around in our seats in anticipation of eating several of those delicious glazed donuts or sweet pecan rolls that the donut shop was famous for serving. She was as sweet as those donuts and pecan rolls, and she knew how to bring a smile to our faces.

In her more recent church life at Starlight Missionary Baptist Church, she was as active and involved as she had ever been. She recorded minutes for monthly business meetings. She coordinated the annual Black History program and the celebration of Dr. King's birthday. She was a member of the Finance Committee, Mission Board, sang in the choir, and was the substitute pianist. The tangible things that she did as a member of Starlight MBC came first from her love for Christ, followed by her love for her church's history and the love of her church family. She did them also because she held Starlight's pastor, the Reverend E.W. Sanders, in high esteem.

She often expressed to me how much he had strengthened the spiritual life of Starlight over the years. He led the effort to remodel the interior of the church, all without incurring any debt. He teaches Sunday School and preaches a strong message every Sunday, not just once a month. His leadership and genuine love for Starlight are evident to regular attendees and visitors. On those occasions when I was in town and visited Starlight, Reverend Sanders called on me to say a few words. Invariably, I commented on his leadership and the love that I felt in that sanctuary. It was the same love and sense of family that I felt as a child sitting with my feet dangling from the pew, listening to inspiring songs, prayers, and strong preaching.

Although Reverend Sanders' place of residence is in a different but nearby city, he tirelessly immerses himself in the activities of the Hattiesburg community. He supports politicians and programs in Hattiesburg that uplift the Hattiesburg community in general, and the black community in particular.

On January 22, 2014, at the march commemorating the 50th Anniversary of Freedom Day, Reverend Sanders, Daisy, and I were proudly at the head of the march, singing freedom songs and feeling the spirit of fallen civil rights soldiers accompanying us in that two-mile march for freedom.

Many of the personal and professional contacts that Reverend Sanders made in Hattiesburg were because of Daisy. She had a steady hand on the pulse of the community and knew the key players in the local religious, political, and social milieus. She took him around town to meet those individuals. As a result, the Hattiesburg community inherited a new activist and advocate in Reverend Sanders.

Reverend Sanders also held Daisy in high esteem, often referring to her as the energizer bunny rabbit. She kept going and going and going. He often said that he has to really plead with some people to do things in the church. With Daisy, however, he had to plead with her to slow down. Reverend Sanders shared with me on a couple of occasions that he noticed that Daisy was slowing down and not quite as spry as she used to be. We both believe that she was aware that she was slowing down because she warned the church leadership that her time was growing nigh and that someone should be preparing to take over for her. Everyone knew that whoever replaced her had to possess a very high level of ability, stamina, and love for the Lord and Starlight. She set the bar extremely high.

Out of his concern for the noticeable change in Daisy's energy level, Reverend Sanders organized an Appreciation Day several months before her health started to deteriorate. He wanted her to have her flowers while she could still enjoy them, he told me. He was very thoughtful, insightful, and prophetic in his belief that Daisy was slowing down and that she should be honored before it was too late. The event took place at Starlight and was well-attended by family, friends, and local politicians. The Mayor honored her with the Key to the City. A steady stream of friends and family paraded to the podium for nearly an hour to extoll her virtues. She received more than an ample supply of roses to smell and appreciate that day. She was bathed in heart-felt sentiments from people who loved her deeply, and it made her full of the joys of spring. My brothers and I will always be grateful to Reverend Sanders and the Starlight family for the love and support they showed Daisy before and during her illness and the outpouring of sympathy and assistance following her passing.

***

Deaconess Peggye Bush, Starlight Missionary Baptist Church

What I miss about Mrs. Wade is seeing and being with her on Sunday morning at Sunday school. As soon as she saw me, she would greet me with a smile and say, "Hi, I am here by the help of the Lord." We would then talk about what happened on the news. Although the news was serious, she would find a way to lighten things up a little bit by saying something funny that made me laugh. We would then start preparing for Sunday school, reviewing the lesson for the day and reading over the scripture. When church started, we both sang in the choir, and to get ready for that, I depended on her to make sure I was on the right hymn, often whispering to each other. That sometimes got Reverend Sanders' attention, and he would give us that look, which told us to quiet down. For some reason, I could not keep straight the songs and hymns we were supposed to sing, so I ended up looking over her shoulder to see what song was next.

When church was over and my husband and I had settled down after a good meal, she would call me and ask if I had my TV on CNN. I usually didn't, so, she told me I should turn to it and watch whatever she was watching. I think that had it not been for her, I probably would not have known what was going on in the country and around the world.

She dressed in her Sunday best. I admired her clothes, and it was clear that she gave careful attention to what she wore. She believed in dressing up for church. She didn't like it when people came to church dressed like they were going to a night club.

I will miss her smiles, her warm greetings in the morning, and most of all, her spirit. Her love for the Lord showed through in everything she did.

***

Mrs. Dora Harris, Sister-in-Law (Read at Daisy's funeral)

Daisy was an extraordinary woman – she had the wisdom of Abigail. She knew her feats and her limitations. She was as fearless as Deborah and as brave as Esther. Not only was she a warrior for Civil Rights – but also for Human Rights – for we all are sons and daughters of Adam the son of God.

She was as caring as Dorcas and as hospitable as Martha. She opened her home to strangers who became lifetime friends and if you were sick or bereaved you received one of her special banana puddings.

She reared three sons and instilled in them principles of love, honesty and integrity – love God, love yourself, and then love your neighbor the same as you love yourself. These principles have been handed down to the grand and the great-grandchildren. Anthony was precise when he said she was the backbone of the family. All these talents combined constitute the character of the virtuous woman in Proverbs 31.

On a personal note: Daisy was my informant – she kept me abreast of the news reports because she knew I would forget to watch. When it was time to go to the polls I would call Daisy to ask who are we voting for. I trusted her judgment.

I had two major surgeries within six months and she was there for me at the hospital and at home during my recovery. We all are going to miss her but not for long for soon and very soon Paul's prophecy will be fulfilled: For the Lord Himself shall descend from heaven with a shout, with the voice of the archangel, and with the trump of God: (No secret rapture) and the dead in Christ shall rise first: then we which are alive and remain shall be caught up together with them in the clouds, to meet the Lord in the air and so shall we ever be with the Lord.

***

For if we believe that Jesus died and rose again, even so them also which sleep in Jesus will God bring with Him our resurrection depended upon His resurrection. As a family we can comfort one another with these words.

Joyce Sanders, Member of Starlight Missionary Baptist Church and wife of Reverend E.W. Sanders

Putting into words what Miss Daisy meant to me is a lot harder than I thought. I have just come to realize that she had become a stand in for my mother. She influenced who I voted for, my opinion of elected officials and how I felt about new legislation. If I wanted to know something, she was my reliable source. Anything concerning civil rights or black history, I depended entirely on her. Although these are important areas of influence, the thing that sticks with me most is that she showed me how to treat people. I watched her on several occasions, with individuals that the rest of society would have turned their backs on, go out of her way to help. The fact that she helped them is not what sticks with me; it is the way she treated them. She made them feel as though it was a privilege for her to help them. I was and am still amazed at the fact that a lady of Miss Daisy's refinement could be so humble, that she made the destitute think themselves to be worthy of her service. She didn't leave them just feeling happy; she was able to help them. She made them feel as though they had done some great deed for her by allowing her to serve them.

Chapter 2
Family

Except for her faith, nothing was more important to Daisy than her family. Her love for my brothers and me was as deep as the ocean, and like the ocean her love never emptied. She loved us unconditionally and totally. Though we loved Woofie dearly, we were much closer to Daisy. And that was mainly because she was the nurturer in our family, a role she relished and played to perfection her entire life. She made sure we were fed, clothed, and churched. She helped with homework, attended PTA meetings, and packed our school lunches. She was an expert at multitasking before multitasking was cool. It was not unusual for her to cook a meal, fold clothes, talk on the phone, and help with homework, all at the same time. And remarkably, but not surprisingly, she did justice to each task. When one of us, most likely Harold, had a cut or scrape that produced blood, she was there with a dab of Mercurochrome, a bandage, and a soothing word to lessen the pain. When one of us, again most likely Harold, got into some mischief, she would dispense punishment while wiping away any lingering tears from his eyes caused by the whacks to his rear end.

She had to keep a close eye on Harold because there was no way of predicting what he would get into. Harold and school were like oil and water. They just did not mix well. If he had had his way, he would have gone to school for one reason—recess! In his desire to skip school one day, Harold lucked upon what he thought was the perfect excuse to stay home the next day. While playing baseball with some friends, Harold misjudged an errantly thrown hardcover baseball. The ball smacked him in the mouth, causing a front tooth to loosen but not to become completely dislodged from his gums. Most people would have cried or at least announced, "I quit!"

Remembering that he did not want to go to school the next day, Harold devised a plan that he thought would surely earn some sympathy from Daisy, and at the same time be the perfect excuse for not going to school the next day. He did not cry, and he did not say, "I quit!" Instead, he called, "Timeout!" We all looked at his mouth and shrieked. He went into the house, found a pair of pliers, and yanked the loose tooth from his mouth. He went back to the game and pocketed the extracted tooth. Later that evening, he showed the upper incisor to Daisy and asked if he could stay home from school the next day.

"My mouth is sore, Daisy, and I won't be able to talk at school," he said.

In her reply to him, he did receive the sympathy that he was hoping for, but to his displeasure, not the reprieve from school that he hoped would accompany the sympathy. She reached out and pulled him into a warm hug. "Come here, baby. Let me take a look at your mouth. Oh, my goodness that looks bad. I hope it doesn't hurt too bad. Let me put some ice on it to bring down the swelling. Baby, I am so sorry you got hit in the mouth with the ball, but you will go to school tomorrow. You don't have a fever and you are not sick," she said.

Of course, that burst his bubble, but it did show her how much he hated school and the lengths he would go to avoid it. It also showed him how serious she was about school. He was reminded that Daisy had a soft touch and a strong spine.

***

Even as she neared her final days, she maintained that nurturing instinct and steady bend toward selflessness for which she was known. In nearly every stage of her illness, she expressed concern about others as much as others expressed their concern about her. Shortly after entering the Windham House Rehabilitation Center, she told me, "Being here for a few weeks will give others a chance to rest." She was referring to the volunteers who came to her house to cook meals, give her medicine, check her glucose, take her to the bathroom and generally provide the care she needed. In her mind, going to the Windham House was not for her benefit. Instead, it was for the benefit of others.

A couple of weeks before she passed away, three of her grandchildren and their mother, all of whom live in other states, visited her at Windham House. They knew how fast her health was deteriorating, and desperately wanted to see her before it was too late. Their visit was at a time when her illness had progressed to the point where she did not always recognize certain people. None of us were sure if she would recognize her grandchildren and daughter-in-law. The four of them waited in the hallway, just outside the physical therapy room, where Daisy was receiving therapy. I entered the physical therapy room and walked over to where she was sitting. I was aware that she was not enjoying herself. Her countenance was low, and she was not smiling. I knelt down to her eye level. As our eyes met, she flashed a warm smile, which I returned. Her smile grew warmer and bigger as she slowly looked passed me and saw her grandchildren, Dorian, Leslie, Jasmine, and their mom, Kay standing in the hallway. At that moment, she burst into tears, not from sadness but from sheer joy of seeing her grandchildren and daughter-in-law. The four of them walked into the room and joined Daisy and me in a big cry as she greeted each of them with a hug and asked, as best she could, how they were doing.

A week later, I visited her at the Windham House after being away for several days. In the span of that week, the stage of her Alzheimer's illness had become even more advanced. Although she was taking medication, the Aricept was not slowing the advance of that horrible disease. Despite the treatments she was receiving, she continued to have conversations with deceased family members, to hallucinate, and not completely swallow her food. When I walked into the facility, I saw her sitting in a wheelchair that was parked next to a couple of staff members who were trying to place the wheelchair on a scale to measure her weight. I walked over to her and placed my hand on her back. She did not respond. Her head remained in a sleeping position, though she was not asleep. I knelt down in front of her and softly spoke her name. She opened her eyes, and they quickly met mine. At that moment she started sobbing.

I asked, "Daisy, are you okay? Why are you crying?"

Her reply was, "I'm just so glad to see you." Needless to say, I cried like a baby. A week later, she was gone.

***

After I was married, Daisy would call me several times a week, just to check on me. "How are you doing, Ant? You need anything?" She did the same for Harold and Junior. I would lovingly tell her that I was fine and that it was not necessary to call so frequently to check on me. However, it was not until after I had my own children that I finally understood why she called. Before I became a parent, her welfare calls seemed so unnecessary — of course I'm okay. After my first child was born it dawned on me why she was so persistent in knowing about my well-being. *Parents never stop thinking, caring, and even worrying about their children from the time they are conceived until they die.* I am eternally grateful that she taught me a very valuable lesson about the enduring power and strength of a parent's love for their children. I have come to realize over the years that while a father's love is potent, there is nothing quite like a mother's love. I also came to realize that the phone calls from her were more for her benefit than for me. Nothing like hearing directly from your children to know that they are fine. Today, I check on my adult children just to hear their voices and to find out how they're doing. I am sure they will do the same with their own children.

***

Woofie proposed to Daisy in late 1950. Having gone as far as the eighth grade, which was the norm for black males in that era, Woofie was

FAITH, FAMILY, FRIENDS, FREEDOM
The Life and Legacy of Daisy Harris Wade

limited in what he could offer her in terms of material things. Daisy had to make a decision between accepting a generous, full-ride scholarship from Alcorn College and accept Woofie's marriage proposal. That decision, she told me, was not that difficult. What made it easy for her were two factors. One, she loved Woofie and wanted to be his wife. Two, she was a bit leery of spending four years in Lorman, Mississippi, about three hours from Hattiesburg, with no transportation, no family, and no guarantee that she would even like college.

An answer to Woofie's prayer for a job that would support him, his new bride, and their baby boy, James, Jr., came when Daisy's father was able to secure a job for him at Hercules Powder Company, a chemical company that was the largest and best paying employer in Hattiesburg for black men. With a steady income, they were able to purchase a home and move out of Daisy's parents' home. Initially, Daisy did not work outside the home. For many years, she was a stay-at-home mom. But as the family grew from one to three, extra income was needed in order to clothe, feed, and maintain a household that had grown to five. A couple of unfortunate miscarriages prevented a bigger increase in the size of the family. In order to help out with expenses, she resumed babysitting for Dr. K.R. O'Neal, Sr., which started after she graduated from high school in 1949. She also took a job as a maid for another white family — the Kelseys — cooking, washing, and cleaning for the family of four. Referrals from Mrs. Kelsey, who lived in the upscale Hillendale neighborhood, allowed Daisy to make extra money working for other white families in Hillendale. For a while, working as a domestic was steady work, but over time, she began to work fewer hours, and eventually she stopped altogether. In addition, the civil rights movement began to steer her away from a life of servitude and toward one filled with the promise of freedom and dignity.

Later, she went to work for WORV Radio Station in Hattiesburg, the first black-owned radio station in Mississippi, serving as receptionist, secretary, salesperson, and on-air personality, hosting a popular, daily gospel music show. For several years, she was a gospel music concert promoter, responsible for bringing to Hattiesburg such notable gospel artists as Shirley Caesar, The Mighty Clouds of Joy, The Gospel Keynotes, The Original Five Blind Boys of Alabama, and Clarence Fountain. After leaving the radio station, she worked for the local television station, WDAM, as a receptionist. She held other jobs over the years, including substitute teacher, sitter for home-bound adults, and home economist for the Mississippi State Extension Service. She retired from the Extension Service after 17 years of service.

***

Although Daisy and Woofie loved each other very much and were committed to a lifetime together, it was not to be. They divorced in 1970, about 20 years after they each vowed to remain married until death did them part. Their breakup was mostly Woofie's fault, a fact to which he grudgingly admitted, being the serial abuser and habitual womanizer that he was. Daisy was aware of his infidelity, but vowed to stay in the marriage for better or for worse, in sickness and in health, 'til death do they part. As in many relationships in which one partner is a confirmed cheater, theirs evolved from verbal arguments to physical assaults. On many occasions, Woofie assaulted Daisy, often in the presence of my brothers and me. In today's parlance, Daisy would be called a victim of domestic violence, of spousal abuse. Usually, a slap with one of Woofie's huge hands across her face was triggered by something as simple as her cooking a meal that he did not like, a response to a statement or question he did not like, or being slightly late picking him up from work.

He had a trigger mechanism that alerted us that his anger had reached a point at which he would likely hit her. He would bounce his leg up and down on the floor, while patting that same leg with his hand. That would be followed by his bottom lip curving under his top teeth. When that happened, all hell was about to break lose. I recall one day he did not like the rice and gravy Daisy had served him. He slammed the plate of food down on to the dining table causing the brown, gravy-covered grains of rice to scatter across the floor. He stood and went into his predictable routine of shaking and patting his leg. He tried to slap her, but because

she was expecting it, she was able to cover her head and face.
He yelled, "You can't do a damn thang right. You know I don't like my rice this chewy. I ought to put something on your ass so you know better next time." He bolted from the house instead, thank God. Daisy was in tears and bawling from fear and anger. I walked over to her and put my arm around her.

"I'll be okay, Ant, Junior and Hal, don't worry, I'm okay. At least he didn't draw blood this time." Junior, Hal, and I helped her clean up the mess on the floor.

On another occasion, he began to beat her with a clothes hanger. That made Harold as angry as a disturbed hornet. As Woofie passed him in the hallway, Harold stood on a table and popped Woofie on the side of his head with a curling iron. He gave Harold a good spanking, one that Harold was proud to take.

Woofie's mother was complicit in one of his physical attacks on Daisy. Mama Mag was at our house during one of those attacks, and instead of trying to get her son to stop beating Daisy, she joined in by hitting Daisy in the head with a shoe.

I was deeply disturbed by the arguing and fighting. I frequently played the role of referee and mediator, even as a young adolescent. Nights when Woofie was not at home and should have been, I spent hours tossing and turning in my bed. Adrenaline was racing through by body. Butterflies were bouncing around inside of me. My rest was uneven and fitful as I listened for the sound of his car pulling in to the driveway. The moment he pulled in to the driveway, my restlessness and anxiety went straight to acute because I knew that an argument would likely ensue. And I knew I might have to go into mediator/referee mode. I knew the drill as referee quite well because I had so much practice. If I heard them talking, I maintained a level of vigilance and alertness that would enable me to hop out of my bed on a moment's notice, if necessary. If I heard Woofie snoring, I knew that he was asleep and that it was safe for me to finally close my eyes and go to sleep. But, if there was conversation coming from their bedroom, I knew their muffled words would very likely escalate to loud yelling and arguing. When they did escalate, that was my cue to race to their bedroom and play my zebra role by pleading with them to stop fussing. I wanted them to stop fussing not only because I wanted so desperately to go to sleep, but I was also so desperately afraid that Woofie was going to strike Daisy or worse.

Daisy eventually grew tired of being a punching bag and began standing up to Woofie, physically and verbally—although she was no match for him. One night, Woofie scared the daylights out of everyone in the house after my pleading fell on deaf ears. On that unforgettable night, he had come home much later than he should have. When conversation led to yelling, I was up from my bed like a jumping bean, and like a referee breaking up a hockey fight, I was between them. Daisy was throwing medicine bottles, ink pens, and a pen cushion at him, telling him that he was not going to get in her bed after being out so late, obviously with another woman. She was angry and hurt.

Woofie sought to put an end to the conflict by announcing, "I know how to put an end to this shit!" I could tell from the sound of his voice and the look in his eyes that this was going to be bad—real bad. He abruptly leapt up from the wooden armchair in which he was sitting, spun around, and moved quickly toward the closet. Immediately, I grabbed Daisy and pushed her down the hallway and out the back door. I knew this was going to be bad because the closet was where he kept his pistol. And based on the sound of his voice, I feared that someone was going to die, maybe all of us. Harold and Junior had also gotten up and joined me in futile attempts to get them to stop fussing, but they did not join Daisy and me in fleeing the house. Instead, they stayed and continued their pleas with Woofie to calm down. They even tried to wrest the gun away from him. In the meantime, I had grabbed a baseball bat and held tightly to Daisy's hand as we rushed out the house in our night clothes.

With my heart pounding like a jackhammer, I listened for the sounds of gunshots as I peered around a corner of the house to see whether Woofie had followed us. After believing the situation had settled a bit inside the house, I told Daisy to stay outside and that I was going back inside. When I walked in, Woofie was straddling Junior's chest, choking, cursing, and warning him to never again get in his face with warnings about not hitting his mother. I was glad Daisy did not witness that scene, or there would have been bloodshed for sure. I walked back outside and told Daisy that we were going to walk to Mama's house, which was several blocks away. I insisted that she stay with Mama that night for her safety. She reluctantly agreed, while expressing concerns about how her three boys were going to be.

The next day, Woofie threw his pistol into the Leaf River. Not only did that incident scare Daisy, my brothers, and me, but it also scared Woofie. Daisy was very fearful that Woofie was going to kill her and maybe the entire family. She cut out stories from newspapers of families being murdered by a family member. And if that was not enough to get my attention, she reminded me about the man who shot his wife and children on Scott Street in Hattiesburg, several years earlier.

Not long after that incident with the gun, I pleaded with Daisy to get a divorce. I told her that I was afraid someone was going to get hurt or killed if she and Woofie stayed together. Although she wanted to keep her wedding vows to stay together until death, the incident with the gun could have tragically marked the end of those vows. She agreed. They separated and eventually got divorced. Both remarried. Daisy's second marriage was also a disaster. She made the mistake of marrying someone who had been a bachelor his entire life and saw no reason to give up his bachelorhood simply because he was married. Not really knowing his personality and values well enough, Daisy had accepted his marriage proposal, married him, and moved to his home in Cleveland, Ohio. She eventually decided that was not the life she signed up for and moved back to Hattiesburg.

A few years after the divorce, Woofie changed his life and became a faithful member of the True Light Missionary Baptist Church. He atoned for his mistreatment of Daisy through confession, prayer, and seeking Daisy's forgiveness, which she readily granted. She forgave him because that is what the Bible told her to do, and also because she still loved him, despite the tumult that characterized most of the twenty years they were married. He and Daisy learned to get along much better after they were divorced than when they were married. Likewise, my brothers and I each established a unique and loving relationship with him as we grew older.

Daisy wanted my brothers and me to have a good relationship with Woofie. Whenever she talked to one of us on the phone, she would tell us, "Make sure you call your daddy and go see him when you come to town." Despite the bitterness and the pain that they both suffered after their marriage failed, she never talked bad about him as a father. She told us that he was always a good father, even if he failed as a husband. She reminded us that as a couple, they both worked tirelessly and with great sacrifice to make sure we were well cared for from the moment we were born.

Today, decades after they divorced, my brothers and I have unique and very precious memories of Woofie. Without qualification, we revere him, love him, and miss him very much. I think that is due in large part to Daisy and also to Woofie and his three sons. She did not like for loved ones to harbor resentments and hold grudges toward one another. In fact, she made sure that my brothers and I stayed in contact with each other, especially after we each married and moved to different parts of the country. She insisted that we not drift apart and that we maintain contact with one another.

Daisy believed in reconciliation and atonement. She not only believed in it, but she also practiced it. How many battered and abused mothers would encourage their sons to have a good relationship with their formerly abusive husbands? Because she was a loving and loved woman, she is among the few who would do so.

Junior and Woofie eventually became more like brothers than like father and son. Woofie spent annual vacations with Junior in Florida, hanging out, and teaching Junior his secrets to perfect barbecuing. I had the unique privilege and blessing of being alone with Woofie when he died of a heart attack March 17, 2002. Harold spent many weekend afternoons hanging out with him and letting him get to know his grandsons.

***

Even with the enormous amount of love she had for my brothers and me, Daisy still had plenty left over for other relatives. Cousins, nieces, nephews, in-laws, grandchildren, and great grandchildren all felt and experienced her love many times. Almost daily, she was on the telephone checking on a family member, while urging them to watch a news story on CNN. It did not matter if that family member was a blood relative, related by a current or former marriage, or lived in Hattiesburg or in some distant place. She made no distinction.

She frequently made welfare calls to Detroit to Joann, Woofie's daughter by his first marriage, even though she and Woofie had been divorced for many years. Although Daisy did not raise Joann or have much contact with her during her early years, she nevertheless regarded her as a daughter. She supported Joann in every way she could, just as if she had given birth to her.

***

JoAnn Harris, Stepdaughter

I first met Daisy at the age of 9 or 10. My Mom would send me from Detroit to Hattiesburg to visit her family. My Dad, James Harris, aka Woofie, would come by and pick me up to go to his house. There I met Daisy and my three half brothers, Jr., Anthony and Harold. I would come every summer until the age of 12.

As an adult I didn't have much contact with Daisy until my Mom passed in

1991. I was about 40 by this time. Daisy started calling me on a weekly basis, and I would call her. She would send Christmas and birthday gifts for me and my daughter. She did that for years. Although she did not have much money, she always managed to send some to me and my daughter. I was struggling and her gifts would come right on time.

One day I asked her why was she sending me money, and she said that when I was little my Dad would give her his whole paycheck for their family and she felt bad about not sending me anything. I told her I appreciated her, but that was really up to my Dad to do that. She said I know, but I wanted to do this. She continued for years doing this.

I always called her my stepmom. We talked religion, politics, and I looked forward to talking to her until she got ill.

She was a beautiful and thoughtful person and she will always have a special place in my heart.

***

Daisy also had regular contact with Woofie's niece, Barbara, who has lived most of her life in Chicago. Before moving to Chicago, Barbara lived in Hattiesburg with her paternal grandmother, who adopted her after Woofie's sister, and Barbara's mother, Helen, passed away. Barbara lived less than a mile from her Uncle Woofie's house, but she had little or no awareness of him, her other uncles, or her cousins. The story Daisy shared with me was that one day when Barbara was walking to school, she passed our house as Daisy was sitting on the front porch. Daisy noticed that the beautiful teenage girl bore a strong resemblance to Woofie's sister, Helen. After a period of time, she was able to confirm that, indeed, this lovely young teenage girl who passed our house every day was Helen's daughter. Daisy persuaded Woofie to reach out to his niece and do what he needed to do to get to know her. Woofie did as Daisy had requested. As a result, Daisy forged a strong relationship with Barbara that lasted until Daisy passed away. After learning of Daisy's deteriorating health,

FAITH, FAMILY, FRIENDS, FREEDOM
The Life and Legacy of Daisy Harris Wade

Barbara telephoned me to tell me that she was coming to Mississippi to spend time with her dear Aunt Daisy. She said that she was coming to help with whatever we needed her for. After learning that Barbara was coming to visit her, Daisy could think of nothing else to talk about for days. Her memory was fading fast, but every day she said, "Barb's coming to see me."

***

Barbara King McKinley (Barb), Niece and Friend

Daisy, a petite, warm, loving woman of God, was dedicated to the intrinsic values of family and loved ones, her church, community, and the entire City of Hattiesburg. To know Daisy was to love her, no in between. Although Daisy was small in stature, she was a powerhouse of facts when it came to politics in Hattiesburg.

Daisy was a walking "Hattiesburg American." Anything you wanted to know about Hattiesburg, just ask Daisy. She loved the City, the Mayor, and volunteered her time for service where ever needed. When she spoke, you listened. She valued justice for all, one of the many causes that keep her engine rolling.

I'm not sure how old I was when I met Daisy. My grandmother told me she was my aunt. She was the prettiest person I had ever seen with long brown hair down to her waist in the back. She was only 10 years older than me. I knew she was my aunt, but because we were so close in age, I looked upon her as a big sister rather than an aunt. She became my idol. I wanted to look like her. I wanted my hair to be long like hers, so I began to brush my hair every night to make it grow longer. It just never happened for me.

I used to walk pass their house on my way home from school. I would see Daisy sitting on the porch when I came home from school. One day I stopped by to say hello. Soon after getting to know my Uncle Woofie, Aunt Daisy, and my three little cousins, I babysat them. I loved sitting with the boys. When she was away from the house, Junior was the man of the house. He was very playful, but always respectful. Anthony was always reading or doing homework. He had a smile and big brown eyes that made you just want to hug him. And Harold, well, you could say that Harold was a little bit of a challenge for me. I really didn't think he liked me at first. One evening, I missed him in the house with us, so when I went to look for him, I followed the smell of cigar smoke. He was on the side of the house trying to smoke a cigar. At first I made him put it out. Then I decided to make him smoke it, with the hope that it would make him sick and that would be the end of his cigar smoking. Didn't happen.

Daisy and I talked about girl things. She talked to me about school and how important it was to set goals for my life. She inspired me to become a teacher. She would take me with her to church. Later in my life, she would take me to see the African American Military Museum in Hattiesburg, the new park, housing, etc. She loved Hattiesburg, and she worked hard for its improvement constantly.

After graduating from high school, I left Hattiesburg and moved to Chicago with my father. She kept up with me. She kept me up to date about the movement. She would send me newspaper articles and photos of the boys. Anything that had to do with the movement and family, she made copies and sent them to me.

She remembered all of the important dates in my life. She never neglected to call me on my birthday. My birthday in 2014 was the first time I did not receive a call in over 30 years.

Daisy was a phenomenal woman. She stood for everything that was legal and the right thing for her family and the people of the State of Mississippi. She volunteered her time with city government. She was a "drum major for justice."

Each time I came home she continued to look out for me. She would make sure I had a car to get around in the entire time I was home.

She loved EURO, and she encouraged me to come back home to celebrate the event. I came whenever I could. In 2013, we sold Anthony's new book **Ain't gonna Let Nobody Turn Me Around,** during EURO registration — we were a team. She took me to the parade and the new park in East Jerusalem Quarters.

We attended the luncheon, the banquet and the ball. She made sure I had everything I needed to have a wonderful time while I was there. She was indeed my big sister, and I loved her dearly.

When Daisy was in the hospital in October, I had to come to be with her. Nothing could stand in my way. I had to be there for her. She knew that I was coming, but she just didn't know when. When I walked into her room, she was telling the nurse all about me.

"That's my niece. She came from Chicago to see me. You know, she was the first Miss Rowan, back in 1959."

I stood behind the nurse; and when she finished attending to her, the nurse turned to me and said, "I hope you are Barb. She's been waiting for you all day." She was indeed very happy to see me. Our visit meant the world to me. We laughed and cried together because we both knew that her journey on this earth was coming to an end.

I knew Daisy loved me because she told me; and she showed me in so many ways. I loved her with every beat of my heart.

***

If a family member needed someone to accompany them to the emergency room or on a doctor's visit, they would call Daisy, and she was there. When her sister-in-law, Dora, was taking her cancer treatments, Daisy often accompanied her to the oncologist. Likewise, after she recovered from cancer, Dora often accompanied Daisy to her doctor's visits. When my cousin Beverly lost a daughter and two grandchildren to carbon monoxide poisoning, Daisy was at the hospital with Beverly and other relatives to lend support in her time of need. When her sister, Emma, was suffering from emphysema and kidney failure, Daisy cooked for her and her children, drove her to the doctor, and gave her emotional support until she passed away. When her brother James moved from Washington, D.C. to Gulfport and spent his final days with his daughter Patricia and at the VA Hospital, Daisy visited him several times a week. When another brother, Richard, moved to the Mississippi Gulf Coast, she spent quality time with him, despite the hour of drive time that separated them. As his health deteriorated, eventually leading to his unfortunate death, Daisy maintained a constant vigil of prayer and visits to his bedside. Although Richard and Floyd had a different father than the other siblings, they maintained a close relationship with each other. Whenever uncle Richard came to Hattiesburg for a visit, he and Woofie spent a lot of time together. Many people actually thought they were brothers because they looked so much alike. When her brother Floyd's health began to deteriorate, she was in constant contact with him and his children at his hospital and home in Washington, D.C. When her late nephew, Maury, was stricken with severe kidney disease, a condition that started when he was a child, she was heartbroken. She drove him or accompanied him to Jackson for his transplant surgeries and follow-up treatments. Over the years, the two of them were in constant telephone contact, each checking on the other. Whenever he came to Hattiesburg from Texas for a visit, he made sure to visit his Aunt Daisy. She frequently rewarded his visits with one of her tasty banana puddings. That alone made the trip worthwhile for Maury. After Maury answered his call to the ministry, their relationship strengthened even more. By long distance telephone they often prayed with and for each other for strength and healing.

When her brother Elbert, who lived in Washington, D.C., was suffering from cancer, she was in constant contact with him and when he passed away in 2006, she went by automobile to his funeral, a distance of nearly one thousand miles. She did the same when Elbert's dear, sweet wife, Rolande, passed away in 2001. I have a special place in my heart for Uncle Elbert and Aunt Rolande. Whenever I visited Washington, D.C., they made sure I was comfortable and safe.

On one occasion, I attempted to take a taxi to their home from where I was staying in downtown D.C. I got into three different cabs before one of them would take me to their house. After settling into my seat in the cab, I told the driver I wanted to go to Ely Place, Southeast. Immediately and as if they had rehearsed identical scripts, they each said that they did not know how to get to Ely Place. I had been to his house many times, so I knew the route to get to his house. I gave them turn-by-turn directions. Take Pennsylvania to Minnesota. *Take a left at Minnesota, and then directly to Ely Place.* They still said they did not know how to get there. I called Uncle Elbert to verify that I had the right address, and he said I did. He was livid and said that taxi drivers are legally required to take customers to any place in the District, no matter where. He said they did not want to drive to southeast because they typically could not get fares leaving that area. At any rate, the Director of Security at the Mayflower Hotel, where I was staying, noticed that I was having difficulty getting a taxi. He asked me to write down the address on a slip of paper he handed me. He went to the next driver in the queue and told him that if he did not take me to that address, he was going to order every taxi driver lined up in front of the hotel to leave. All of a sudden, the next driver remembered how to get to Uncle Elbert's house. Daisy was always happy when I visited Uncle Elbert, Aunt Rolande, and their children — Bobby, Simone, Belinda, and Monika. Uncle Elbert and his family were pleased with the visits as well. Although I was unable to attend Uncle Elbert's and Aunt Rolande's funerals, I thought so much of them.

When Daisy's sister, Louise, was in the emergency room following a near fatal car accident, Daisy was right there with my Uncle Luther and the rest of the family praying for her healing and recovery. When my brother Harold had open-heart surgery, two months before her death, Daisy was at the hospital every day until he was released.

***

Regina Mims, Niece

Aunt Daisy was one of the most beautiful and nicest women that I had ever seen. Being the youngest of my Mom and Dad's union, I didn't get to experience her as much as the rest of my siblings. The first time that I really remember seeing her was during a visit that she and her boys made to Chicago where we lived after we moved away from Washington D.C. After that, seeing her and the boys usually happened during a few summer trips to Hattiesburg. She had a beautiful, warm smile and such a pretty face; and I would just sit and stare at her sometimes and occasionally play with her hair. I loved her hair!

The main thing that I remember is when I started my career as a Flight Attendant in 1979. I would fly mostly domestic trips at that time and when I talked to my Father about a trip that I had coming up he would make sure that if I was traveling to a particular city that I would have the phone number of any relatives that lived there. I don't recall the year, but it was sometime in the early eighties that I finally got a trip with a layover in Cleveland where Aunt Daisy lived at the time, and I called her. They would pick me up at the airport and drive me to the house where she would have the best home cooked meal you could ask for. We would sit around and talk and laugh or watch TV, and then I would go to bed that she had fixed up for me that was far better than the hotel beds that my fellow crew members were sleeping in that night. Sometimes if I didn't have to leave too early the next day, she would make breakfast for me also. They would drop me off at the airport, and I would get on the airplane bragging to my coworkers about my Aunt Daisy and the food that I had the previous night. This would happen a few more times. At the time, I wasn't married, didn't have children, and didn't see my family as much as I would have liked. So, seeing a familiar face and getting a home cooked meal was always, always appreciated. I will always remember her for that.

***

Debbie Holmes, Niece

My aunt Daisy Harris Wade has been a Godly influence in my life. One of the first things that come to mind is that she was a woman of courage as evidenced by her involvement in the Civil Rights Movement.

She deposited within me memories of her selflessness. She was a giver and a woman of compassion. She gave of her time, her God given gifts and resources. For example, my paternal grandmother, Lennette Hayes, was in a nursing home *for many years. Daisy visited with her regularly and reported her condition to my parents not by their request but by her own volition. I was so impressed by that…especially when I learned that she visited many others with the same level of commitment.*

Daisy was very intelligent and seemed to know everything! Many times, she would be the first person to inform me of newsworthy, historical, political and social events. However, one of my fondest memories is about a time when she didn't know about something. Daisy visited us on a holiday which happened to fall on a Sunday. She attended our church service, but left quickly at its conclusion to help my mother finish our holiday meal. I didn't tell her that a popular pastor who had recently divorced his wife was planning to get married that day, after our church service. Some might have considered this a scandalous event because he married a member of his church. I didn't tell anyone about it because I was told that the ceremony was private. I could hardly wait to tell my family when I arrived at my parents' house, after the wedding. Daisy was speechless after hearing my announcement! After a moment of silence, I remember hearing her release a piercing shrill. Then she said, "Why didn't you tell me!!! I would have stayed for that wedding!!!" That was the only time I remember her yelling at me. I smile every time I think about how Daisy reacted to not knowing something.

I am grateful that God placed her in our family. My aunt Daisy, a woman of wisdom, courage & compassion continues to influence me today.

***

Daisy was a straight shooter. No one ever had to guess or wonder what she believed or how she felt. She let them know in no uncertain terms about how she stood on a particular matter. In doing so, she made no distinction among family or friends when she thought someone's thinking or behavior needed correcting. For example, most mothers take up for their sons, even if they are wrong. There is something about a mother and her male children, especially black mothers and their black sons. But for Daisy, if you were wrong, you were wrong, no matter who you were.

And she did not mind letting you know. When my brother James was having marital problems with his first wife, Daisy did not reflexively take up for him, no matter how much she loved him. In fact, she confronted him and told him very directly and forcefully that he was messing up. She warned him that he was going to lose something very special if he did not change his ways and stop disrespecting his wife with his stupid behavior. She was right, but he did not realize it until it was too late. Despite the breakup, Daisy maintained a beautiful relationship with her daughter-in-law, Kay, never referring to her as her former daughter-in-law.

***

CHILDREN

Daisy had a special place in her heart for the little ones, whether they were kin or not. She was motivated to do so, in large part, by two scriptures: *And he said: Truly I tell you, unless you change and become like little children, you will never enter the kingdom of heaven. (Matthew 18:3). And he will answer, 'I tell you the truth, when you refused to help the least of these my brothers and sisters, you were refusing to help me (Matthew 25:45).* She was also motivated because she genuinely loved children. In her heart, she considered children vulnerable, innocent, and often in need of special help. She readily agreed, for example, to work at a local school as a substitute teacher for special needs children, although she had no special training. What she had instead was a big, loving heart, which went a long way in meeting the needs of those special babies as she often called them.

Charles Street, the street next to her house, was one of the routes school children took when walking to school. Every day she watched them as they passed her house, keeping a sharp eye out for anyone misbehaving. She was not afraid to deliver a stern lecture to one of them, if they were saying or doing something she considered ugly. She did it out of love, not meanness. She mainly did it as part of her obligation as a member of the village to help instruct and guide the children toward a positive path.

On those occasions when there was rain, she showed her love for the traversing school children in a much different manner. When she spotted them from a block away, she walked outside underneath the carport and waited for them to get close enough to speak without raising her voice. She offered, and they eagerly accepted, towels with which to dry off and clean mud from their shoes. That tiny, but very powerful gesture, spoke of her genuine love for the little ones and her deep Christian faith to take care and protect *the least of these*. I also imagine she was prompted by a memory from her own childhood when some adult offered her a towel to wipe away the water and mud from her shoes. She was passing along a tradition that had been handed down to her through the generations from her ancestors — *take care of one another*.

Not one to just know that a problem existed, she was about doing something to fix the problem. While she was at the Windham House, she asked me to call the Mayor to request that something be done about the muddy pathway the children had to take as they walked to and from school on rainy days. She told me that she intended to make the call herself, but her illness had prevented it. The Mayor asked me to pass along to her his thanks for bringing the matter to his attention.

Children at church looked forward to seeing her each Sunday when she would reward their good behavior with a stick of gum, a lollipop, or a candy bar. Grandchildren and great grandchildren loved to drop by her house for a visit. Besides wanting to see Grandma Daisy, they were anxious to see what goodies she had waiting for them — cookies, cake, ice cream, and the healthy stuff as well — collard greens, baked chicken, and sweet potatoes. By responding to someone else's needs, and yes, sometimes their wants, she was Daisy being Daisy. That was especially true when it came to babies and children.

Daisy's sister, Louise, shared a story with me about the three sisters when they were in their teens that highlighted the relationship among the three girls. Daisy, Emma and Louise had chores to complete after dinner and sometimes before dinner such as washing dishes, setting the table, and helping with the cooking. One Sunday afternoon, following super, Emma and Louise were anxious to get to the movie theater in time to get good seats. They were attired in their Sunday clothes and were feeling excited about making the two mile walk to the movie theater and getting their popcorn and finding good seats before the movie started. Daisy was several years older than they were, and many times she assumed the role of second mother and taskmaster.

As Louise and Emma were about to push open the front screen door to start out on their trek to the theater, Daisy yelled, "Mama, Emma and Louise are trying to leave the house and they didn't finish cleaning up the kitchen!"

"Y'all ain't going nowhere 'til y'all get back in that kitchen and clean it up. And I mean it better be clean," said Mama. Alas, Emma and Louise missed the movie, but learned that big sister Daisy was not going to give them any slack when it came to doing their chores.

***

Harold Harris, Jr., Grandson

My grandmother was the definition of a giving lady. She was so selfless, always looking out for other people. If you were sick and couldn't count on anybody else to come and visit you, she would without a doubt, bring a card, or a banana pudding, and if you were lucky, you would get both! Even if she were feeling under the weather herself she would still be there. Even as my granny was sick, she still looked out for her family. As her dementia worsened, she NEVER lost her giving spirit. When the staff at Windham House would bring her lunch or dinner, she would take a few bites then say, "Wrap this up and save it for those kids when they come".

I started staying with her 2 years before she passed away. She knew me, and very well at that. Whenever there was something wrong with me, she knew. I'm not sure whether it was the grandmother in her or just her instinct, but every time I was broke, she knew. Maybe it was my facial expression that gave it away, but EVERY TIME she would manage to slip me something, even if it was only five dollars. She would give her last for her family to be happy. No matter what I did, right or wrong, (I always felt I was right) she was in my corner to encourage me to not let my mistake hold me back and keep pushing on. She always wanted me to go back to school. She would always tell me that can't nobody take that piece of paper (Diploma) from you once you get it. I'm glad she had the chance to see me get registered to go back to school. She was so excited. Even when she was sick, before I would go to class, I would tell her to have a good day. She would respond, "Bring me back some good grades." I will never forget the things my granny instilled in me.

***

Valencia Harris, Granddaughter-in-Law

I could barely remember the first time I met Mrs. Daisy Harris-Wade, who quickly became known to me as Grandma Daisy. My boyfriend and self-proclaimed favorite grandson, Stephon, invited me to accompany him to a program at Starlight. I think it was a Martin Luther King program. I agreed to go along and the beginning of her profound impact on me started that day. She stood up to speak and told the story of her sons being on the Picket Lines and her memories of Martin Luther King coming through Hattiesburg. She spoke with such passion about her accounts and it made me self-evaluate my own life. From this point on, I had the opportunity to visit and chat with Grandma more and more frequently because I became engaged to her grandson and shortly after married into the family.

I cannot even remember what the beginnings of my relationship with Grandma Daisy were like because she always made me feel so welcomed in her presence. We would talk about gardens and good, country eating (some would call soul food). She would tell me short stories of her historical encounters in the city of Hattiesburg. We would pick her up for trips to Gulfport and back. She would talk to me about landmarks and people she knew as we drove along. Even in our casual conversations, there was a voice of passion. I could feel her strong *sense of fondness for the strides that had been made in our history and her genuine care for all people. Although sometimes my attention may have been diverted, I would reflect on our conversations and think of the drive she had to educate people, particularly the younger ones of us coming along.*

She loved and cared for her family so much. She was constantly sending food to our house and buying and giving things to the children. She was so very thoughtful. She remembered our birthdays and we could be sure to get some type of gift just to know that she thought of us. Perhaps the most memorable gift for me would be the card and one-dollar bill she gave my husband for his 31st birthday. Although we laughed a bit at the idea of a dollar for a thirty-one year old, I couldn't help but also feel touched because of her giving heart. No matter the cost of the item, she seemed to have a deeper understanding for what it meant to make an impact and touch the lives of those she came into contact with.

Even now, I walk through my house and find reminders of her love and generosity, from the silverware in the kitchen to the socks my children may wear to school in the mornings. Although we were not blood-related, Daisy Harris-Wade was my grandmother, too. She would call to check on me more often than I checked on her. I would think to myself, this should be the other way around.... I'm the younger one and I should be checking on her. I can remember just before she hung up, she would say, "Okay now, I'll check you later, you hear?" Even as we left her house after a visit, this is what she would say. I could go on and on just thinking of our different conversations and opportunities I had to spend time with her. However, I can sum it up and say she influenced me to have more passion about life's opportunities and inspired me to leave a stronger, more intentional legacy. It was very evident that she was driven by her faith, motivated by her family, liberated by her freedom, and dedicated to her friends. When I grow up, I hope to be as inspiring to those around me.

***

Jasmine Coicou, Granddaughter

Growing up and spending summers in Mississippi there are a few things that I will never forget. Granny displayed how important it is to be well rounded. She played the piano and was very involved in church, she visited the sick, she didn't miss a funeral, she worked with the developmentally delayed, she worked with Eureka/Rowan, she loved her trips to the coast with friends and she absolutely loved everyone in her family no matter what. I strive to be that selfless and giving daily. She made it look all so easy because she was passionate about it.

I remember just a couple of years ago we arrived to Hattiesburg and within 20 minutes of being there Grandma had snuck away for a moment and she came out to the front fully dressed. We asked her where she was going and she said, "I just saw an obituary in the paper of someone that I know and saw that the funeral starts in about 30 minutes so I'm going to go. I'll be back."

I thought to myself, "Now we just drove ten hours to see this woman and she is taking off already," and then I quickly remembered that she was all about being there for others and paying respects to those that went on.

Before passing, Grandma told me to do all that I can for other people. Gosh, that has stuck with me since the moment she said it because she lived it, and I know she meant every part of it.

I am so thankful that when my parents split, Grandma didn't take sides and put us aside. She was so determined to keep us in her life and our family member's lives. She loved my mother just the same and always maintained a supportive relationship with her. I'm forever thankful for her taking us for the summers to give my mother a break and through those summers, my life was totally shaped in many areas in great ways.

When I miscarried back in September of 2013 grandma was one of the first people I wanted to talk to because she knew that pain oh too well. She told me, "It's okay. Your time will come. Don't you stay down about this. God is going to bless you. Don't stress about it."

And I felt a weight lifted. Her words and tone were so soothing and positive. I knew at that point God was speaking to me through her. Now I am 5 weeks away from delivery date, 4/26, and I would be elated if she came on 4/22, Grandma's birthday. My life has been enriched because of simply being in her presence and her not only telling me right from wrong, but living it.

Faith, Family, Friends, Freedom
The Life and Legacy of Daisy Harris Wade

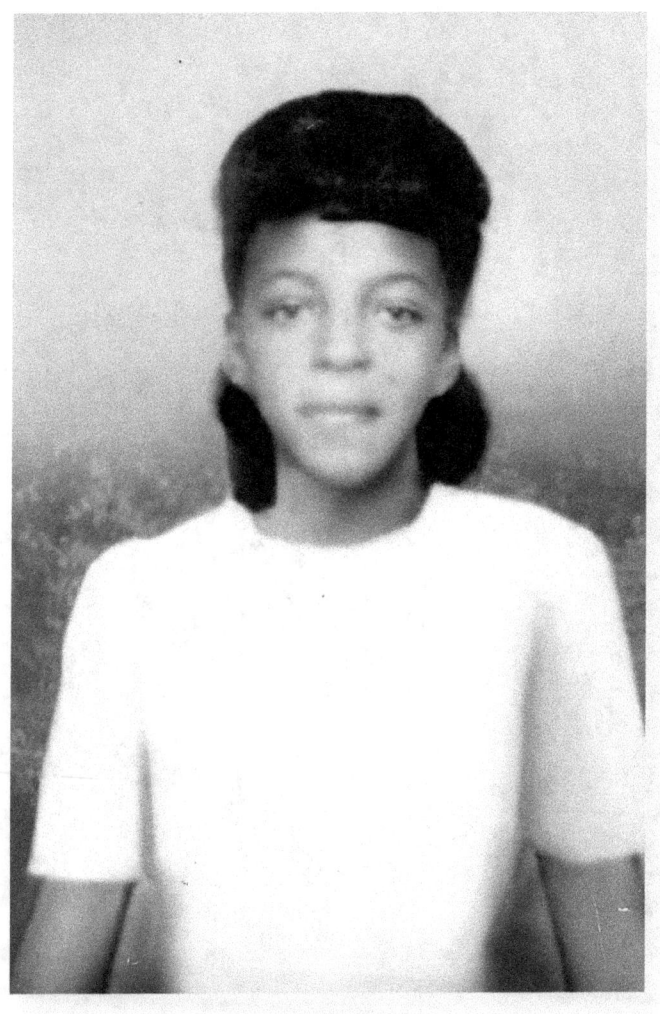

Faith, Family, Friends, Freedom
The Life and Legacy of Daisy Harris Wade

Faith, Family, Friends, Freedom
The Life and Legacy of Daisy Harris Wade

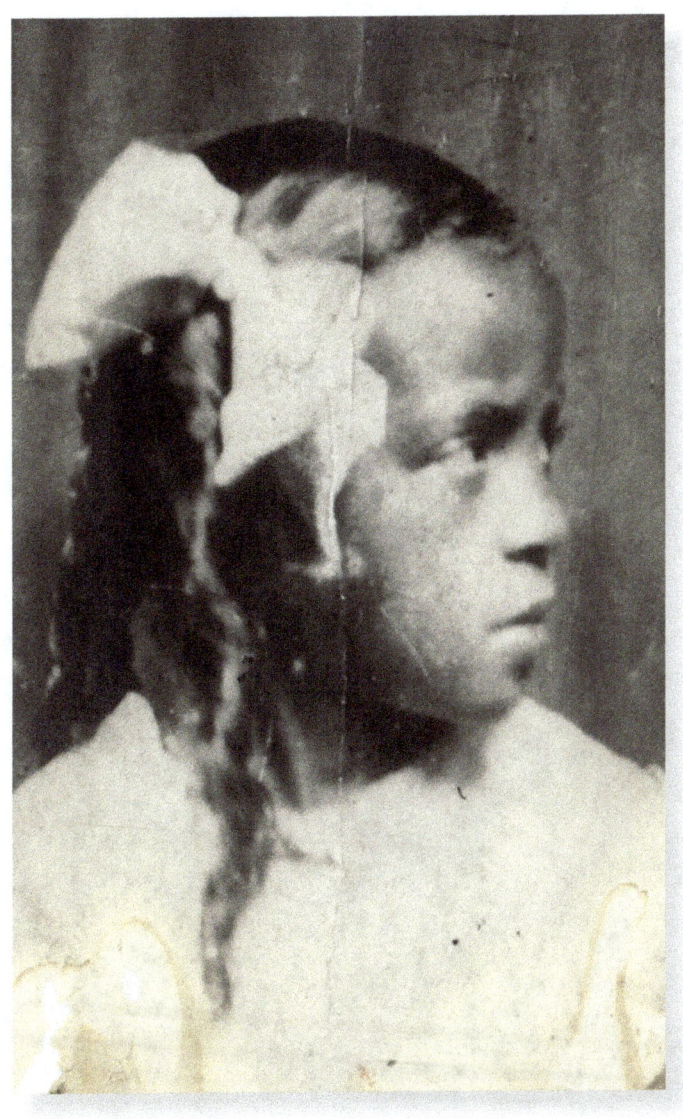

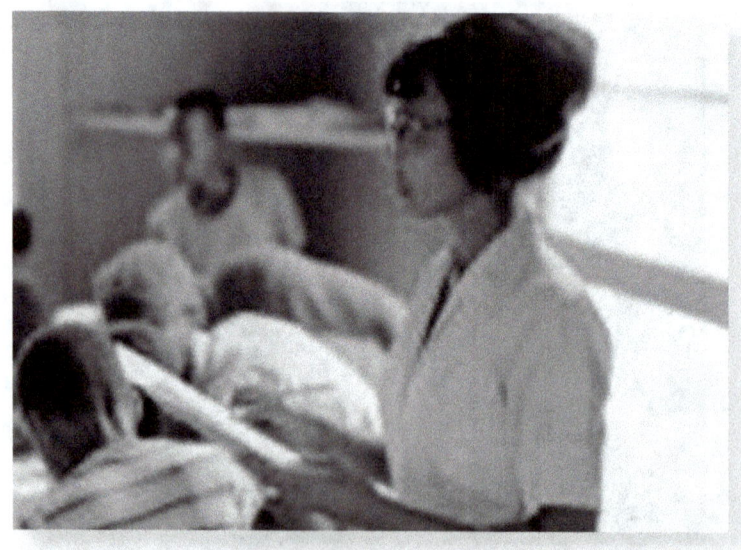

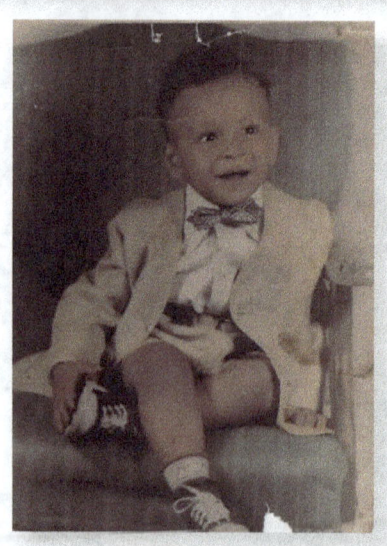

Faith, Family, Friends, Freedom
The Life and Legacy of Daisy Harris Wade

Faith, Family, Friends, Freedom
The Life and Legacy of Daisy Harris Wade

Faith, Family, Friends, Freedom
The Life and Legacy of Daisy Harris Wade

FAITH, FAMILY, FRIENDS, FREEDOM
The Life and Legacy of Daisy Harris Wade

Faith, Family, Friends, Freedom
The Life and Legacy of Daisy Harris Wade

FAITH, FAMILY, FRIENDS, FREEDOM
The Life and Legacy of Daisy Harris Wade

Chapter 3
Friends

Daisy counted among her friends, many members of her family. And she counted as members of her family, many of her friends. Such is evidence of how much she loved and cared for her family and friends and how she made little distinction among any of them. Her circle of friends was wide and inclusive. The color of a person's skin, religious background, gender, or income was not a criterion for being in her circle. She unconditionally accepted people for who they were, not for who she wished they were. It included blacks and whites, blue collar, white collar, pink collar, or no collar. Her friendships were permanent. Once someone became her friend, they were friends forever. The only time she referred to a friend in past tense, was after that person died.

And she had a knack for making me acquainted with her friends, especially those who lived in other states. Whenever she knew that I was traveling to a city where she had a friend, she insisted that I call them. Not one to rely on her memory or the telephone directory, she kept a notebook filled with names, phone numbers, and mailing addresses of her friends and family, locally and in other states. After giving me the person's contact information, she would spend time giving me the details of her life long relationship with the person. So, before I contacted them, I already had a pretty good idea who they were, based on all of the background information Daisy had given me. I got to know several of her friends and family members while on business trips. I became acquainted with her friends, Della Mae and Pluke, when I traveled to the Oakland, California area. When I traveled to Washington, D.C., I became more acquainted with my Uncle Elbert, his family and with one of her closest and dearest friends, her sister-in-law, Tina. When I traveled to New York, she made a point to give me Paula's phone number. When I traveled to Detroit, I checked in with her cousins.

Daisy was from an era when friendships were valued and not taken for granted. She and her friends seemed to have a bond that was as strong as hemp rope and resistant to pettiness and jealousy. I am sure they had disagreements, but they also knew how to ask for and accept forgiveness. People from Daisy's generation just seemed to operate with an attitude about friends and family that is discernibly different than that of the current generation. I guess that is partly because they all grew up when relationships were far more important than things. Their friends were real, not virtual. They actually talked to each other, rather than communicate through emails, twitter, and text messages, thereby making communications, both verbal and nonverbal, clear and unambiguous. As children, they played outside, got into arguments and fights, and learned the art of forgiveness and making up. They played with real people rather than with animated characters and avatars on a computer or television monitor. They learned that words and actions have consequences, and cannot be purged with the stroke of a key on game console or computer keyboard. They all grew up in the same poor economic conditions, which enabled them to see how much that had in common and not what was different about each other.

The following is a list of Daisy's really close friends, although the list of friends and acquaintances is too long to include. The point of including these names is to acknowledge and honor Daisy's friendships that I personally know about.

Delores Thigpen—Lois was like a second mother to my brothers and me. Her children—Ronnie, Cheryl, Renee, Valerie, and Mike were like our brothers and sisters. Our home was their home, especially when annual floods forced them and Ma Moore to abandon their home. Lois and Daisy remained very close, even after Lois moved to Los Angeles. Lois passed away in 2007.

Bobbie Jean Smith—I have such fond memories of Bobbie Jean. She was a very beautiful woman, who had two children, Madelyn and Tony, both of whom were close in age with Junior and me. She and Daisy were high school classmates and remained close through adulthood, until a car accident took Bobbie Jean's life during a trip to Hattiesburg from Chicago, where she had relocated.

Louella Harris — Punkin, as she was called, was Bobbie Jean's younger sister. It seemed like Punkin and Daisy spent hours talking on the phone and visiting. If Daisy was talking on the phone, there was a good chance that Punkin was on the other end. I have this very vivid memory of Punkin and her husband, John, accompanying Daisy and Woofie to the Royal Social Club Ball and Dance one year, when I was a young child. There is a picture they took of Daisy and Woofie, decked out in their formal evening wear. They looked so happy together and of course, I thought that no one at the Ball could be prettier than Daisy. After Punkin passed away, Daisy remained friends with John and their daughter Deidra. John and Daisy were CNN buddies. They both constantly watched CNN and called each other when there was a story they thought the other should see. At John's funeral, Daisy spoke fondly of their CNN friendship. Most people at the funeral chuckled because their CNN viewing was legend.

Sondra Doss — Sondra was the youngest sister of Bobbie Jean and Punkin. She and Daisy were as close as sisters. They talked by phone or in person on a daily basis. Sondra's husband, Perry, was also very close to Daisy.

Madelyn Johnson — Madelyn was Bobbie Jean's daughter. Daisy and Madelyn were constant telephone partners. After Madelyn's stroke, Daisy was there for her, taking her food, driving her to doctors' appointments, and giving her words of encouragement during her rehabilitation. When Daisy's health began to deteriorate, and she needed someone to provide daily care, Madelyn was the first person to offer her help. And every day, until Daisy went to the Windham House, Madelyn was at Daisy's house cooking, giving her a bath, and helping her dress. There was just something about Bobbie Jean's family that attracted Daisy to them and they to her.

Fannie Griffin — Tina, as she was known, was Daisy's sister-in-law and very close friend. She was married to Daisy's brother, Eugene or Bay-Bay as he was known, who died after serving in the U.S. Navy. Tina grew up in Hattiesburg, but has spent most of her life in Washington, D.C. Daisy and Tina were constant telephone buddies, and once or twice or year, Daisy flew or took the train to visit Tina. I was at Daisy's house one evening after Daisy had been admitted to the hospital. The telephone rang, and it was Tina. She had been calling Daisy for several days and leaving messages. She told me that she was worried because she was not able to get in touch with Daisy. I told her about Daisy's illness and she was heartbroken. As Daisy's health worsened, I called Tina to give her regular updates. The hardest call I made was to tell her that Daisy had passed. When she answered the phone, she sensed something foreboding. I could hear it in her voice when she said hello. Before I could tell her that Daisy had passed, she said, "Oh, my God. Anthony, don't tell me." I told her that I was sorry to tell her that her friend was gone.

All she could say was, "No. No. She can't be gone. No, Anthony. Don't tell me that."

Dorothy Jean Griffin — Dorothy Jean was married to Daisy's brother, James or Frenchie as he was known. Daisy and Dorothy Jean called one another every day for years. Daisy's death was a huge blow to Dorothy Jean. My brothers and I visited her after we were told that she was taking Daisy's death very hard. Her hurt was very evident as she cried uncontrollably the moment she saw us.

Alice Fluker — Alice was Daisy's comrade in arms during the civil rights movement. Their friendship started when they were little girls.

Janice Anderson — Janice and Daisy had a hotline between them. They lived on opposite ends of their block on Fredna Avenue. If they were not talking on the telephone about something on CNN, they were alerting each other about some impending danger or cause for concern on

Fredna Avenue.

Dedra Harris — Dedra is Punkin's daughter. After Punkin's death, Daisy maintained a close relationship that was both sisterly and maternal. Dedra loved Daisy and her death was a huge hurt for her.

Dora Harris — Dora and Daisy were married to two brothers, Harold (Sonny Boy) and Woofie. They were more than sisters-in-law. Dora was a friend and a source of spiritual strength for Daisy. Daisy drew from the incredible strength that she showed during her successful battles with cancer.

LaVada Frazier — Mrs. Frazier to me. She is my mother-in-law. Theirs was a very special relationship that went beyond being in-laws. They spent hours on the telephone talking about topics ranging from children to church. They were both blessed with the gift of carrying on conversations for hours without stopping. Althoug they saw each other maybe 3 or 4 times face-to-face over the last 38 years, they gave each other comfort and telephone companionship they both cherished.

Barbara McKinley — Barb was Daisy's niece. She was a very special person to Daisy, ever since they met when Barb was in high school. Daisy beamed with pride when Barb was named Miss Rowan during her senior year of high school. There was a difference of only about 10 in their ages. So, they were more like friends than like aunt/niece. They established a loving friendship that lasted decades.

Donald and Sun Core — The Cores and Daisy became close friends after the birth of Bianca, Daisy's first great grandchild. They are parents to Eboni, Bianca's mother. They loved Daisy and treated her like she was family, though they were not related, neither by marriage nor blood.

Barbara Johnson — Barbara was a close friend, who was also Daisy's supervisor with the Expanded Food and Nutrition Education program. Barbara and Daisy maintained a very healthy personal relationship despite their professional relationship. Barbara was younger than Daisy but had more professional experience in the field. She mentored Daisy and provided the training she needed to be a successful agent. She encouraged Daisy to enter her banana pudding in a local baking contest. To no one's surprise, Daisy won the blue ribbon.

Beverly Jones — Beverly was Daisy's niece and constant phone buddy. They checked on each other several times each day. Daisy had a special bond with all of Beverly's children and grandchildren. Whenever any of them were in her presence, they treated her like she was their mother.

Mildred Johnson — Mildred was a friend from childhood. When she and her family moved away, she and Daisy remained in constant contact with each other. As Mildred's health deteriorated, her children would call Daisy to give her updates on her friend's health.

Eloise Huddleston — Eloise and Daisy were first cousins, but their relationship was more like sisters. I remember Eloise, in her younger days, as a talented cook and hairdresser; and she still maintains her cooking talents. She owned her own beauty shop and restaurant. As she aged, Eloise's health declined. Daisy visited her nearly daily to check on her and run errands for her.

***

After Daisy passed away, the family received phone calls, emails, cards and letters from her friends, many of whom I had never met or heard of. They were from both new and old friends, people who felt the sting of her death, but also felt blessed to have known her. A sampling of those mostly hand-written words of sympathy shows just how much her friends and family loved her.

I will always remember her as a sweet angel with a smile on her face. As we were growing up she opened her doors to us and made sure everybody was ok. To Bro.

Harold and the rest of the family, stay strong and continue to trust God.

Mrs. Harris was a lady of strength and purpose. Hattiesburg is a better place for its citizens to live, work and play because of Ms. Harris. She was relentless for the underserved and left out and she never gave up fighting for justice and equality. It scares me to know that only a few Soldiers of her kind remain with us. Thanks to the family for allowing her to serve humanity with her enormous gifts. Heaven has gained a hard worker. We lived among Harriet Tubman's heir and history maker.

What an example for all of us in this community. A woman of virtue whom I have always respected from a little girl. God bless you all and I pray the peace of God be with you always.

My sincere condolences the Harris family. She will be truly missed. Be proud of the great life she lived and the lives she touched.

Praying God will comfort you and give you strength. You have many good memories and life lessons taught by a strong woman who loved people. Be Blessed!!

As I was flying down to Mississippi to attend Aunt Daisy's services, I was listening to music on my iPod and staring at this page trying to gather my thoughts and find words of comfort to write to you, the original version of **It's So Hard To Say Goodbye To Yesterday** *by G.C. Cameron came on and my first thought was "how appropriate." I know that your hearts are heavy and that they will be for a while. Aunt Daisy was a beautiful person inside and out. I would like to dedicate this song to you and hope that you will take comfort in the lyrics. I couldn't have said it better. Aunt Louise, I would also like to dedicate it to you for I know that your heart is heavy also after losing your sister. May you all find comfort in knowing that Aunt Daisy was loved and will be missed by so many for a very long time.*

Your mother will be missed. She was a good friend of my late mother.

Daisy was like a second Mom to me. She was my stepmom; however, she treated me like part of the family. I remember when I was about 9 visiting MS and going to the house on Fredna Avenue. She was a great lady and will be missed by all. Love you Daisy.

Ms. Wade will truly be missed. She was a beautiful person inside and out.

Growing up white in MS during the Civil Rights era, I was grown before I understood the courage and sacrifice required to establish these rights for all. Praise God for leaders such as your mother who were determined to see all treated with equality and dignity and respect. My prayers are with her family and with our community. We have lost a true hero.

The laughs, the smile, stopping by to check on me, sitting on the front porch, the phone calls, endless conversations, these are the things I will miss from my very true, best friend, and classmate.

A special lady has passed through and left her footprints, now she's in Heaven.

Anthony, so proud to see your mother on the PBS Special.

Your mother was an extraordinary person. I felt like my life was touched by the stories and the history she lived.

Her obituary was a fascinating tribute to a life well lived.

You are richly and forever blessed to have such an amazing mother.

***

Cheryl Moore Outlaw, Family Friend

Daisy Lee Harris Wade has been a part of my family's life for as far back

FAITH, FAMILY, FRIENDS, FREEDOM
The Life and Legacy of Daisy Harris Wade

as I can remember (since I was born). I remember the devastating floods of 1961 in Hattiesburg; the army trucks were going around the black neighborhoods picking up what we called refugees. Daisy insisted we come to live with her and her husband and three boys in a three bed room house on Fredna Avenue. We were nine strong cuddled up with each other and as happy as a lark. We went every day to see how high the water had gotten (as children this was the highlight of our day). Daisy would cook breakfast, fix lunch and we always had a hot supper. We stayed with the Harris family for a couple of weeks (until the water went down and we were able to clean the mud and dirt from our house). Even though my mother (Deloris) and Daisy had been friends from their teenage years, that flood brought us all together as one big happy family. In fact, Lois and Daisy were inseparable. When you saw one you saw the other.

Daisy used to tease us about our hair and skin color. She would say both families are so messed up with one dark skinned with long pretty hair, the other bright skinned with nappy hair. We wondered what must we do. We laughed all about the skin color and hair joke. Eventually, my mom moved to Los Angeles, CA to further her education in nursing. Daisy came out there a few times, but my mother would come home every summer and they would hook up for the summer. After my mother's husband died, it was a matter of months before she moved back to Hattiesburg, Daisy had divorced her husband and Lois lost her husband in death, so now the two were together again, just the two them. Excitement filled the air every day. Daisy would come to Lois's house and Lois would come to Daisy's house (Daisy did most of the cooking). They would have someone drive them down to the coast almost every weekend. This didn't last long, money for gas, eating out; spending unnecessary money was wearing out.

Now the news begins to be the hot topic every day. They both knew what was happening all over the world with just one phone call, that's all. WDAM, MSNBC CNN, WLBT, and any other news station. Daisy would call Lois up and they would talk about those white republicans and they never used SUNDAY SCHOOL words when they talked about them (they hated FOX). My mother passed away on May 2, 2007 and there was not one day Daisy left us alone. She quickly became the mother of eight children instead of three, Junior, Ronnie, Anthony, Cheryl, Harold, Renee, Valerie and Michael. Harold and I would race to Daisy's house when she would be cooking collard greens, ham hocks, and banana pudding (from scratch). He would be in Gulfport, MS and I would be across town 3 or 4 miles away. She would also bring banana pudding to my school so that the younger generation would know what food from scratch tasted like.

I would always copy information for Daisy about civil rights. She would often say, "Cheryl, please don't let Junior and Hal throw my paperwork away. Make sure Anthony follows up and take care of all my hard work."

I promised her I would tell Anthony to store all of her work in a safe place. I used to think of Daisy and Mississippi History doing the civil rights era. She had the answer to every question young people asked. They would call her from far and near to gather information about the civil rights movement and BABY she had ALL the answers. Daisy went to every black person's funeral whether she knew them or not. She would visit the sick in the hospital or retirement home, go to their houses cook and clean for them. She was a true statue in all of the communities in Hattiesburg.

She LOVED her Mayor and would fight to the end for him (Mayor Johnny Dupree)

I will miss a very fine and gracious lady. Daisy has helped me cope with many things in life after my mother passed away. She taught me and charmed me with her wisdom. Harold and his family spent Thanksgiving and Christmas with us and I am sure Daisy and Lois were smiling and saying this is what it's all about.

***

James A. Hicks, Friend of the Family

When I think of Daisy, WOW!! There is so much that can be said but the most important thing that can be said is that she was just that, MOTHER. Though she bore sons naturally of her own, she birthed many sons & daughters through her

Heart Flame which is where LOVE is housed. When you were in her presence, you were her child. Whatever dictionary you find in the world, when you look for a definition of Mother, true Mother, her name will be among the Greats. As I travel about the country and other places, I often tell people that I was raised by many Mothers & Fathers and Daisy & Woofie take their rightful place in my life right along beside Ms. Annie Mae & Mr. Aaron, who birthed and fathered me. For those of us you parented and schooled, saying "thank you" is inadequate, but along with living our lives with some dignity and integrity, we hope we bring honor to your name and memory, regardless of the paths we've chosen.

May the Source of all creation Mother, Father, GOD-ONE forever bless you wherever your soul resides in the universe for surely your contribution to life qualifies you to reside in a higher plane of consciousness and dimension than that you struggled to help us overcome and to reach for higher planes of being.

***

Robert Lee Trotter, Family Friend

Ant, your mother was a humble woman, who picked me up off the ground & gave me shelter, love, and most of all, true friendship. She was my second mother, who loved me more than my first.

Daisy took me under her guided wings as a child when everybody else in Hattiesburg turned their back on me. I will be reunited with Miss Daisy in Heaven. I share your grief and the loss of your Daisy. My tears today are for the passing of Miss Daisy.

I lost one of the most caring black women on earth. With the passing of Miss Daisy, she is in God's mighty hands now. Soon, I will come home to see her.
Yes, I am taking the loss of Miss Daisy very hard as if she was my own mother. Junior, Ant and Harold, we lost our best friend temporarily until we see her again in HEAVEN. I love you Miss Daisy very much. You made me very proud to be a black man.

Ant, without your mother's love I would not be the man I am today. She helped raise me to become a God fearing, real man. I thank you, Lord, for having Miss Daisy in my life.

***

Georgia (Sallye) Hammond, Lifelong Friend

I first met Daisy at Eureka High School. She was in the 12th grade and about to graduate. I was in the 10th grade and about to go over to the new high school, Royal Street High, as it was known in those days. My 10th grade class was the first class to enter the new school.

One day, at Eureka, I went up to Daisy and asked her to be my "play" sister; and being Daisy, she said yes. And that is how our friendship began. I had to pass her house every day to catch the bus on Main Street for school (Royal Street). We would talk for a few minutes on my way home. Some months later, Daisy became the musician for the Junior Choir at Star Light Baptist Church where I was a member. She and I had good times going over songs, laughing, and talking. Those were the good days of our childhood.

When I finished high school, I got married and moved to California. I spent a few years there before returning to Hattiesburg. Our friendship picked up as though I had never been away. I got a job at the University of Southern Mississippi (USM), and through Daisy's encouragement, I became the 1st black woman supervisor in housekeeping. Daisy was really happy for me. We hugged, prayed, and cried. What a blessing she was!

Daisy went with me for my eye surgery, back surgery, and during the illness and death of my mother. She was an example of a friend, a very good friend. She was loved by my entire family.

The evening before Daisy passed, Alice and I went to see our friend Daisy Lee Griffin Harris. I talked to her as I did every day when she was at home. I was saying my goodbyes to my sister in Christ, my best friend, Daisy. There will never be another like her. Goodbye, my friend.

Anthony, this is for you. A friend called me to talk about Daisy and to try and lift my spirits. This is what she told me:

She and another friend of Daisy went to visit Daisy at the Windham House. They were talking quietly when they became aware of Daisy's laughing and giggling. They asked her let them in on it. She told them very loudly, "No!" Then she kept saying, "God has his arms all around me. I'm wrapped up in his arms." The other friend wept but felt relief that Daisy knew she was in the arms of the Lord.

CHAPTER 4
FREEDOM

In addition to her boundless devotion to her faith, family, and friends, Daisy was irreversibly and doggedly devoted to her freedom. Her yearning for freedom was unquenchable. Once she decided to immerse herself—mind, body, and soul—into satisfying that yearning, she was not going to be content until she and others tasted the sweet nectar of freedom, no matter how long it would take. The defiant and venerable lyrics from that old freedom song, *Ain't Gonna Let Nobody Turn Me 'Round,* became her daily mantra and enduring sources of strength and motivation for her.

Her fight for freedom took several paths, but mainly it was through her involvement in the local civil rights movement. Her service to the movement included serving as Secretary for the Forrest County Branch of the NAACP; volunteering with Student Nonviolent Coordinating Committee (SNCC) and Council of Federated Organizations (COFO); being a co-founder of the Forrest County Action Committee (FCAC); providing lodging for ministers during Freedom Day in the winter of 1964; providing lodging for student volunteers for Freedom Summer in the summer of 1964; driving voter registration canvassers to different parts of town; preparing meals for hungry marchers; arranging bail for marchers who were arrested; helping devise strategies for a successful economic boycott; participating in numerous marches, demonstrations, and pickets, locally and in other parts of the state of Mississippi. Such are examples of the tangible, visible contributions she made to the movement. Beyond those contributions, she provided many intangibles—moral strength and support; hair-raising prayers for the movement's leaders and followers; words of encouragement to fellow foot soldiers in the struggle; and words of wisdom to young people who lacked appreciation for the long, hard slog that was and is the fight for freedom.

In 1963, two tragic events catapulted her into the civil rights movement in Hattiesburg. The resulting decision to become involved in the fledgling movement was not made lightly and without genuine fear for her safety and that of her family. Yet, the assassinations of Medgar Evers in Jackson, Mississippi and President Kennedy in Dallas, Texas in 1963 sparked something inside of her. She saw those two tragic events as undeniable proof that evil forces in our country were at work in a sinister ploy to continue and deepen the oppression of black people. And as such, she decided to join the growing number of black people all across the South, who were sick and tired of being treated as second class citizens, and sick and tired of being sick and tired. In their efforts to silence the movement and its leaders with bullets and bombs, the enemies of the movement, instead, motivated people like Daisy to fight back.

She, like most black people in the South, saw in President Kennedy a friend of black people and a God sent ray of hope. President Kennedy expressed through his words and deeds a desire to end poverty and racial discrimination in the South. That spoke directly to the hopes and aspirations of black people in the South. No other president before Kennedy had shown such empathy and support for poor and black people of the South, although Eisenhower was admired by black southerners for his efforts to end racial segregation at Central High School in Little Rock Arkansas in 1957. In 1963, President Kennedy federalized the Alabama National Guard to enforce a federal court order to allow the first black student to enroll at the University of Alabama. He telephoned Coretta Scott King to offer his support, following a highly publicized arrest of Dr. King in October of 1960. One of the results of that telephone call was Kennedy receiving 70% of the black vote, resulting in his victory in the 1960 Presidential Election over Richard Nixon. And in 1961, Kennedy ended discrimination in federal employment when he established the President's Committee on Equal Employment Opportunity (PCEEO). In the homes of many black people all across the South, including my family's, pictures of Jesus Christ, Martin Luther King, Jr., and President Kennedy hung on walls and rested on mantles. They were our heroes. Jesus represented salvation, and Dr. King and President Kennedy represented hope for a better future.

Medgar Evers showed enormous courage in the face of vicious and repeated threats on his life from white supremacists; and he was a hero to many who admired that courage. So, when Medgar Evers was assassinated on June 12, 1963, Daisy reacted with fervor and determination to take up his battle in her own way, in her own town. I have this very vivid mental image of Daisy sitting alone on our front porch the morning after Mr. Evers was assassinated. She was sobbing uncontrollably with her face buried in her hands. Through those gushing tears and the bolts of anguish that seemed to consume her, she was at a loss. She did not what to say or do except cry and pray, both of which were in ample supply. Beyond the tears, anguish, and sense of loss, a fire was burning inside of her. In her belly was an inextinguishable fire that roared and grew as she found more and more strength and courage to do her part for the fight for freedom. Ain't Gonna Let Nobody Turn Me 'Round! She committed herself to doing what she saw as God's calling for all Christians: fighting injustice and resisting evil, wherever they present themselves. She saw plenty of evil and injustice in the hearts and minds of those who wanted to kill our leaders and to deny basic freedoms to black people, for no other reason than the color of their skin. Moreover, she was motivated to get into the fight for freedom because of her belief in that time honored adage, God don't like ugly!

One of those ugly moments occurred when the anti-civil rights forces in the South hatched a despicable and illegal plan that was designed to impede the progress of the civil rights movement at best and to destroy it at worst. In their way of thinking, this strategy was the proverbial magic bullet that would surely bring about the demise of the movement. This was their strategy: With the complicity of sympathetic state and local governments, the anti-civil rights forces filled the jails to capacity with demonstrators in an attempt to remove from public view the optics of bloody and violent reactions from police that greatly enraged the nation. The strategy assumed that with no demonstrators, there would be no demonstrations; without demonstrations, there would be no media coverage; and without media coverage, the movement would die. That was their strategy. The counter strategy among the civil rights leaders was quite novel and profound. It was to boldly place children in demonstrations and on picket lines, in place of the jailed adults. And in doing so, the civil rights leaders dared the police and firefighters to treat children in the same manner they had treated adults—beatings with Billy clubs, vicious attacks from police dogs, and high pressure water hoses used as weapons on peaceful demonstrators. The images of black children being beaten with Billy clubs, attacked by police dogs, and hosed with high pressure water hoses were not going to sit well with the American public. So, in response to that strategy, local municipalities passed ordinances that made it illegal for anyone under the age of 18 to participate in demonstrations or walk picket a line. The City of Hattiesburg was one such municipality. Thus, a high stakes chess match between pro-civil rights and anti-civil rights forces was in play.

One Saturday morning, in defiance of that ordinance, Daisy took my brother James, my friend Ratio Jones, and me—all under the age of 18—to the Forrest County Courthouse to walk the picket line. We were there under the watchful eye and supervision of Lawrence Guyot of SNCC. Not long after being on the picket line on that cold, wet, January morning, two Hattiesburg police officers spotted us, and pulled up to the curb next to the sidewalk where my brother, Ratio, and I were peaceably walking with handwritten picket signs hanging loosely around our necks. The officers angrily confronted the three of us, yelling to us that we were under arrest for violation of the ordinance that prohibited us from being there. The officers then forcefully ripped the picket signs from our necks and threw the three of us into the back of the police car. Shivering from the cold and the fear, I was living my worst nightmare. Fear, however, immediately took over as the main cause of my shivering as the officer in the front passenger seat put his police radio microphone to his mouth and asked, "Headquarters, have the dogs been fed today? You say they haven't? Well, I'm bringing in fresh meat for 'em." To say that short radio transmission scared the three of us to death would be putting it mildly.

Once inside the Hattiesburg City jail, these three, young, frightened "lawbreakers" were taken to an interrogation room, where the same front passenger seat officer kept up his attempts to frighten and intimidate us. My main concern at that point was being able to detect the sight and sound of hungry, snarling police dogs. But that concern was quickly replaced by another equally paralyzing fear as we sat on the cold, wet, cement floor, with our backs pressed up against the cold, wet cement wall.

The officer unexpectedly plucked a blackjack from his back pocket, tossed it slowly from hand to hand, and moved menacingly in our direction while saying, "This is what we use to beat niggers' asses with."

I thought to myself, my God, apparently we managed to not get eaten by the police dogs, now we are going to die a bloody death at the hands of this mean, crazy policeman. About that time, the door to the interrogation room opened with a loud thud. In walked this small, petite black woman, wagging her finger and yelling to the top of her lungs, "You let these boys go right now. You have no right to hold them. You hear me? I mean let them go RIGHT NOW!"

That was Daisy Harris, coming to the rescue. I had never been happier to see my dear Daisy. We were finally seeing a friendly face. But more than a friendly face, this was justice incarnate coming to stamp out evil. Up to that time, all the faces we saw and voices we heard, wanted to either feed us to the police dogs or bash our heads in with a blackjack. After listening to her righteous rant, the officer did the same as we kids did when she raised her voice: Do exactly as she said! So, he let us leave with Daisy, believing that he had made his point in scaring the daylights out of three innocent children whose only offense was peaceably exercising their right to protest.

There are so many things that stand out for me in that incredibly harrowing experience at the Hattiesburg City Jail. Perhaps, the most amazing things were that Daisy never knocked on the door of the interrogation room; and she never asked, "May I enter?" And she never asked, "Would you please let these boys go?" By bursting into that interrogation room, without knocking on the door, without asking for permission to enter, or without saying please let the boys go, Daisy placed the safety of her children and their friend above her own. She could have been jailed, beaten, or worse. But in her heart and mind, two of her babies were being unjustly detained in that jail, and only God and the cops knew how they were being treated. As any mother would do when their children are in danger, she took unflinching, selfless actions to protect us. She was not going allow her children to be mistreated, especially by someone who was probably a Klansman masquerading as a police officer.

When I reflect on the experience of her willingness to sacrifice her own safety for the sake of my friend, and my brother and me, I automatically think about the story of the Samaritan, the Priest, and the Levite. When the Priest and the Levite refused to render aid to the man who had been beaten and robbed, they were acting out of fear and selfish concern for their own safety. They reasoned that if they stopped to help the injured man, something bad could happen to them. They were afraid that they could also be beaten and robbed. In other words, they placed their own safety above that of someone who was in desperate need of care and attention. The Samaritan, while traveling the same road from Jerusalem to Jericho, took pity on the man and gave him the assistance he required. The Samaritan, unlike the Priest and the Levite, was motivated by something godlier and more powerful than fear and selfishness. Instead of asking himself, "What will happen to me if I stop and help this man?" the Samaritan asked, "What will happen to the man if I don't stop and help him?" I am certain that Daisy had a similarly godly and visceral reaction as the Samaritan. Instead of thinking about what would happen to her if she intervened in that travesty at the jail, she thought about what would happen to her two boys and their friend if she did not intervene. I will always be grateful that she acted like the Samaritan and not like the Priest and the Levite.

***

Daisy was fighting for her freedom during the winter of 1964, when she and Woofie agreed to house ministers, who traveled to the South to assist with black voter registration. The ministers were sponsored by the National Council of Churches and included priests, rabbis, and protestant ministers of various denominations. The clergy members were planning to be in Hattiesburg for Freedom Day, January 22, 1964 to engage in a series of marches and demonstrations for voting registration rights. Instead of a single day with a single march, Freedom Day morphed into a series of daily marches from Mobile Street to the Forrest County Courthouse that went on for several months.

By providing housing for the ministers, my parents were taking serious risks, including possibly being beaten, shot, fired from their jobs, or worse. They balanced those risks with the awareness that the fight for freedom was not going to be free of risks, threats, and dangers. They accepted the notion that if ministers and clergy, strangers in this dangerous and oppressive land in which they lived, were willing to accept risks for our freedom, they could do no less. So, Daisy provided a warm bed and tasty meals for several ministers who lived in our home for several months. They forged a relationship that emboldened them and helped them to appreciate the dangers they all faced in challenging the Jim Crows laws of Mississippi. They were also able to appreciate the notion that despite the dangers, God was on their side, and they were on God's side in this struggle.

Freedom Day was followed by Freedom Summer. In 1964, Freedom Summer brought to the South hundreds of black and white college students, ministers, and entertainers to assist with the struggle for freedom. Freedom Summer, under the leadership of Bob Moses, established Freedom Schools in Mississippi; conducted voter registration drives; helped organize the racially diverse Mississippi Freedom Democratic Party (MFDP); and assisted with plans for MFDP to challenge the all-white regular Mississippi Democratic Party for recognition at the Democratic National Convention in Atlantic City, New Jersey in August of 1964. Daisy and Woofie, at Daisy's urging, agreed to house two white college students—Paula Pace and Beth Moore for the summer. As was the case with housing the ministers for Freedom Day, there were risks involved in housing white civil rights workers for the summer. And just as with the reasoning they used to justify housing the white ministers, my parents realized that if these young people were willing to risk their freedom and their lives, they were morally obligated to do no less.

Fear of losing one's life was palpable when James Chaney, Andrew Goodman, and Michael Schwerner went missing on June 21st, and more so when their bodies of were discovered in Philadelphia, Mississippi on August 4th. Goodman and Schwerner, like Moore and Pace, were white northern college students who responded to the call to fight racial injustice in Mississippi. With their deaths, everyone, including my parents, more fully appreciated the dangers of working for freedom in the state of Mississippi. But by that time, the Freedom train had left the station, and there would be no turning back.

One night, the two white college students living with us, Beth and Paula, accompanied Daisy to Starlight for an evening worship service. Beth and Paula sat at the rear of the church, huddled together, whispering, and gazing at the entrance of the church. Daisy gestured for them to join her at the front of the church, but they did not budge. After a few more gestures from Daisy and refusals from Beth and Paula, Daisy got up from where she was sitting and walked back to Paula and Beth. I was thinking, boy, are they in for it! Daisy asked them why they insisted on sitting in the rear of the church. They looked at each other and then to Daisy. "We want to see the Holy Ghost when it comes in!"

Daisy chuckled and informed them, "Baby, you can't see the Holy Ghost. It's not going to walk in these doors. The Holy Ghost is something you feel when you are singing, praying, and praising the Lord!"

"Oh!", they replied in unison. I think Beth and Paula were a little disappointed and maybe a little relieved at the same time. What would they have done if they had actually seen a ghost walk through the doors, as they had expected?

Daisy's commitment to the struggle was tested in an unexpected and major way. Daddy, Mama, and my Aunt Emma had come to live with us in 1965 after a loan company foreclosed on their house. Daddy was confined to his bed, suffering from severe kidney failure. Each day, the life of this dear, precious man, one of my heroes, was slowly slipping away. One day, he called Daisy to his bedroom and told her to sit next to him on his bed. I was with her when she went in to see him.

"Daisy Lee, I want you to promise me something."

"Yes, Daddy. What is it?"

"I want you to get yourself out of that mess. That civil rights mess. Ain't nothing but bad gonna come from you being in that mess. It's dangerous, and I want you to promise me that you gonna get yourself out of it."

With tears welling up in her eyes, she told Daddy, "Yes, sir. I will." But she knew and I knew that she was not going to "get of that mess", as Daddy called it. She promised she would, but deep inside she knew it was a promise she could not keep, and one that God would not mind if she didn't. She said yes, for Daddy's benefit. He needed the comfort of knowing that his oldest daughter was not going to get hurt or killed because of her involvement in the movement. He knew from living in Mississippi his entire life how vicious and hateful some white people acted toward black people, even before there was a civil rights movement. He knew of the numerous lynchings, beatings, and arrests that black people suffered, with no opportunity to protest or challenge them. So, his request to her to end her involvement in the movement was out of an abundance of caution, safety and concern for her. He was not opposed to the movement. Rather, he was justifiably concerned that his daughter would end up like one of those black people who went missing and was never ever heard from again. Needless to say, Daisy did not end her involvement in the movement.

Another event also challenged her and nearly rocked her to the core. This challenge did not come from some racist out to harm her. Instead, it came from within the movement. As Secretary to the Forrest County branch of the NAACP, Daisy was a member of the Executive Committee. One of the tasks of that committee was to recommend strategies to the community for carrying out and strengthening a fledgling economic boycott. Many white merchants and business owners refused to change their racist hiring practices and the practice of treating black shoppers as less important than white shoppers. In response, the NAACP launched a boycott of those businesses. Slowly, some of the businesses began to change their practices, but most did not.

A difference of opinion developed within the Executive Committee regarding whether the boycott should end with only a few business changing their racist practices or stay the course. Some argued that victory should be declared and that we should be happy that some progress was made. The others countered that now was not the time to let up on the gas pedal. They argued that much work remained and that ending the boycott too soon would accomplish very little. Buoyed by the success of forcing a few obstinate business owners to change their hiring practices and the way they treated black customers, Daisy, Alice Fluker, Mr. J.C. Fairley, and the Reverend J.C. Killingsworth, also members of the Executive Committee, argued for the continuation of the boycott. Their votes outnumbered the few who wanted to end the boycott. In response, the President of the Forrest County Chapter of the NAACP, who was on the losing end of that vote, petitioned the NAACP National Office to suspend the four members from the Executive Committee.

Mr. Roy Wilkins, Executive Director of NAACP, sent a letter dated January 25, 1968 to the Daisy, Mr. Fairley, Mrs. Fluker, and Reverend Killingsworth, informing them that they were temporarily suspended pending a full hearing. On February 8, 1968, Daisy received a letter from Mr. Gloster Current, Deputy Executive Director, requesting that she appear at a hearing on February 17, 1968, 11:00 to respond to charges of conduct "inimical to the best interest of the NAACP." Following the hearing, in which neither side ceded any ground, Mr. Current announced his decision. He would uphold the suspension. Daisy told me that she expected an adverse decision, but that she and the others would not let that deter them in their more aggressive fight for justice and equality in Forrest County. Indeed, it did not. In fact, the four of them formed a new organization—The Forrest County Action Committee (FCAC).

In addition to the four suspended NAACP Executive Committee members, the membership roster of FCAC included Mr. James Earl McGee, Mr. Major Pugh, Mr. Paul Stewart, Mr. Henry Murphy, Mr. James Nicks, and Mr. Charles McArthur. Feeling unencumbered by what they viewed as the tepidness of the NAACP, members of FCAC continued to lead the economic boycott; and they achieved far more success than had their efforts remained under the auspices of the NAACP.

On the heels of her involvement in the Civil Rights Movement, Daisy continued to give back to the community. Not that she thought that the movement was over, she chose to expand her community activism to include other civic activities. She was appointed by the Mayor of Hattiesburg to serve on the City Election Commission. In that role, she was responsible for selecting and training precinct poll workers in her Ward, whose job it was to ensure that proper and lawful voting procedures were followed. In that role, she found herself in a familiar role that harkened back to the days of the civil rights movement.

While going about her duties of counting votes in the mayoral election, a representative of one of the candidates attempted to bully her by raising his voice and insisting that she follow his instructions rather than the instructions supplied by the Mississippi Secretary of State. The confrontation had very clear racial overtones to it. The bully was a conservative white man who represented the white candidate. The other candidate was black. Captured on video on shown on the local evening news broadcast, Daisy got in his face, pointed a finger, and said, "You will not intimidate me. Some of the meanest white folks Forrest County has ever produced tried, and they did not succeed. And neither will you.

Do I make myself clear?"

He got the message and quickly changed his tune and tone. Daisy received numerous plaques, certificates, and recognitions for her many years of community service and activism. At her home going service, November 5, 2014, Mayor Johnny Dupree read the following proclamation, which perfectly summed up her life:

MRS. DAISY HARRIS WADE

WHEREAS, Mrs. Daisy Harris Wade was born Daisy Lee Griffin in Hattiesburg, Mississippi, April 22, 1931 to parents, Annie B. and Joe B. Griffin; and graduated from Eureka High School in 1949; and

WHEREAS, she and James Harris, Sr. raised three boys – James Jr., Anthony, and Harold – and instilled in each of them solid Christian values; and

WHEREAS, Mrs. Wade gave her life to Christ at the age of 15 when she joined Starlight Missionary Baptist Church, where she remained a faithful member for sixty-nine years; and

WHEREAS, her Christian values led directly to her involvement with and participation in the local Civil Rights Movement, including Freedom Summer, COFO (Council of Federated Organizations), NAACP (National Association for the Advancement of Colored People), SNCC (Student Nonviolent Coordinating Committee), and FCAC (Forrest County Action Committee). She participated in numerous marches, boycotts, pickets, and direct actions during the 1960s and 1970s as a loyal and dependable foot soldier in the struggle for civil rights; and

WHEREAS, following her active days in the civil rights movement, she continued her civic involvement by serving as election commissioner and received awards and recognitions from the City of Hattiesburg, Alpha Phi Alpha Fraternity, and Delta Sigma Theta Sorority for her community spirit and leadership; and

WHEREAS, she was a loyal and dependable friend to many, bringing comfort to the sick and bereaved with a kind word, a phone call, or one of her famous banana puddings; and

WHEREAS, she leaves a legacy that will endure for generations, through her impact on her family, friends, community, and church.

Now, therefore, I, Johnny L. DuPree, Mayor of the City of Hattiesburg, Mississippi, do hereby proclaim the day of November 5, 2014, the day of her homegoing celebration, Mrs. Daisy Harris Wade Day

_____

Johnny L. DuPree, Ph.D.

Mayor, City of Hattiesburg

***

The right to vote and the duty to vote were two sides to the same coin in Daisy's eyes. She had very little patience for someone, who was eligible to register to vote and chose not to do so. She heard all of the excuses…I don't have time; I will get to it tomorrow; or I might lose my job. Those were lame excuses, and she had no patience for such nonsense. She reminded them of the long list of martyrs who gave their lives so that they could exercise their right to register and vote—Vernon Dahmer, Medgar Evers, Jimmie Lee Jackson, James Chaney, Andrew Goodman, Michael Schwerner, Wharlest Jackson, Reverend James Reeb, Reverend Bruce Klunder, Mrs. Viola Liuzzo, and Dr. Martin Luther King, Jr. Shame on you, she would say to slackers, for disgracing the legacy and memories of those brave men and women who paid the ultimate price so that you could have the right and duty to vote. And shame on you, she continued, if you are just too lazy, too scared, or just don't give a damn. Securing the right to vote, she said, carried with it the responsibility and obligation to those martyrs to go to the polls on Election Day and cast a ballot, even if your only option is choosing between the lesser of two evils. For many years, that was indeed the reality black voters faced in the South — choose between two people who had very little day light between them when it came to the race issue. Daisy faced that dilemma many times. Whenever she did, she just held her nose and marked her ballot for the lesser of the two evils, while never considering the option of not voting at all.

That reality changed in a very substantive way when black office seekers offered clear choices. When Johnny Dupree ran for Mayor of Hattiesburg, she was absolutely ecstatic to know that her vote helped elect him to that office on three occasions. However, she reminded the Mayor that he should never forget those civil rights foot soldiers whose commitment to the movement in the 1960s is directly responsible for his election some forty years later. Naturally, he heeded her advice on several occasions following his elections.

She felt so incredibly blessed that she had a clear-cut choice in every presidential election since 1960. Her candidate did not always win, but she felt good that she had a choice between two people with vastly different political beliefs — Kennedy vs. Nixon; Johnson vs. Goldwater; Nixon vs. Humphrey; Nixon vs. McGovern; Carter vs. Ford; Carter vs. Reagan; Mondale vs. Reagan; Bush vs. Dukakis; Clinton vs. Bush; Clinton vs. Dole; Bush vs. Gore; Bush vs. Kerry; Obama vs. McCain; and Obama vs. Romney. And like most black people in this country, with the opportunity in 2008 to elect the first black president of the United States of America, Daisy was downright giddy, exclaiming that she never thought that she would live to see a black person elected to the highest office in the land. Tears filled her eyes when President-elect Obama appeared before a throng of supporters in Chicago on the night of his first victory. And when he won again in 2012, in another landside, she felt that finally the hard work and sacrifices that she and others made in that long, hard, and ongoing struggle for justice and equality were beginning to pay off. For Daisy, the elections of Mayor Dupree and President Obama meant that she could finally pass the baton of freedom on to a newer generation. She was satisfied that she had remained faithful, held tightly to the baton, and never wavered.

Closely aligned with her strong views on civil rights were her equally strong views on politics and political parties. Daisy was an unapologetic, unabashed, lifelong, dyed-in-the-wool, yellow dog Democrat. That was a description she proudly embraced; and she epitomized the meaning behind the term, yellow dog Democrat. The term refers to someone who would rather vote for a yellow dog than for a Republican. She viewed the modern Republican Party, the party of Limbaugh, Nixon, Reagan, Bush, Romney, and the Tea Party as hostile to the civil rights movement, and thus to black people in general.

She remembered the efforts by President Kennedy and President Johnson to end racial discrimination and poverty in the South. She remembered that southern white Dixiecrats and Democrats, who later became Republicans, maintained a resistant and hostile attitude toward racial equality. They opposed the Civil Rights Bill of 1964 and The Voting Rights Act of 1965. She remembered that Ronald Reagan intentionally selected the Neshoba County Fair in Mississippi to launch his presidential campaign in 1980. Of course, Philadelphia, the site of the murder of the three civil rights workers in 1964, is the county seat of Neshoba County. She also recalled the white southern strategy Richard Nixon employed in 1968 to entice disenchanted white voters to abandon the Democratic Party and switch their loyalty to the Republican Party. The reasoning behind the strategy was that because so many white southerners were angry over the passage of the Civil Rights Act of 1964 and the Voting Rights Act of 1965, the Republican Party would feed that anger and racism and let them know they were welcome to join their party. It worked, and the demise of the Democratic Party in Mississippi began and has continued unabated since 1968.

In her view, the Republican Party had been openly disrespectful and hateful toward President Obama. They and their supporters had created racist cartoons and caricatures that questioned the President's birthright, education, and religion. She felt that raw racial animus was behind those attacks on the first black president of the United States. Further, she believed, the Republican Party has led the social justice counterinsurgency that is designed to erode the civil rights achievements of the 1960s, through voter suppression laws, United States Supreme Court decision to invalidate a key part of the Voting Rights Act, and gerrymandering efforts that have had the effect of reducing the voting power of black voters.

She was proud to say that she never voted for a Republican. In fact, she never wanted anyone to even think that she was in any way affiliated with the party or any of its members. That was made abundantly clear following the filming of her interview for the PBS documentary, Freedom Summer, in February 2013. The film producers secured what they considered the perfect venue for conducting the interview. They located a large, white, antebellum style home that was located a few miles from Daisy's home. It was clear why the producers selected that home. The interior of the home was the perfect setting for the interview, with hundreds of books perfectly shelved in the floor to ceiling bookshelves, dark wooden walls and upholstered furniture that complemented the rest of the house's Old South decorum.

When she and I drove up to the house, it occurred to her that the house belonged to Dave Ware, the white, Republican opponent of Mayor Johnnie Dupree, the black, Democratic, mayoral candidate. She informed the producers of the ownership of the house and the efforts of the home's owner to unseat Mayor Dupree. The producers did not know about the local political landscape when they secured the house for the filming. Their original site was damaged in a tornado that roared through Hattiesburg a few weeks before. So, she gave them a pass on selecting that particular house. But as she was leaving the house following the filming, she placed a scarf on her head that completely obscured her face. When I asked her why she was wearing the scarf, she said, "I don't want anyone to see me leaving his house and think that I am here to support Dave Ware."

***

Because of her vast knowledge of and experience in the civil rights movement, Daisy was frequently invited by professors at the University of Southern Mississippi and William Carey University to speak to their classes about the civil rights movement in Hattiesburg. She enjoyed telling her stories, knowing that by doing so she was continuing the hallowed tradition of oral transmission of our people's history. She felt that it was important for young people to know about the struggle for freedom, especially from someone who was not only present during that time, but more importantly was also active and in the trenches during the struggle. Reading about the movement is necessary but not sufficient when it comes to knowing the truth about it. The truth emerges when the words and stories of the people who were actually there are heard.

She was also anxious to share her stories because she was sick and tired of seeing and hearing people come out of the woodworks, with bold claims of what they did during the movement. She was there at every significant moment in the movement in Hattiesburg, and she knew full well who did and did not participate in that movement. If you wanted to see her get her dander up, let her hear someone lay claim to having been present at mass meetings, marches, and demonstrations, but who, in fact, was nowhere to be found. Furthermore, she was bold enough to tell that person to their face and anyone else in earshot, that they should stop exaggerating and lying about their involvement in the movement. She became incensed and indignant when Johnnies-come-lately attempted to co-opt the movement and lay claim to its heritage and legacy, when in fact, they were afraid to show their faces at a mass meeting, march, or demonstration. Decades later, when the risks, dangers, and threats have long passed, so many of them feel it is now safe to insert themselves into the history and legacy of that historical movement. Unlike the civil rights Johnnies-come-lately, the legitimate civil rights warriors were brave, courageous, and committed individuals, who were willing to lay down their lives for freedom, justice, and equality.

For anyone who was not fortunate enough to hear her stories directly from her, the following sources are recommended.

1. The PBS **American Experience** documentary, *Freedom Summer*.
2. http://video.pbs.org/video/2365264557/.
3. http://www.lib.usm.edu/legacy/archives/m334.htm?m334text.htm~mainFrame
4. http://www.crmvet.org/info/hburg.htm
5. Personal papers and photos maintained by her sons.

Conclusion

Faith, Family, Friends, and Freedom, the passions and priorities that drove her actions, decisions, and beliefs. They kept her focused on what was important in her life. As critical as they were, those priorities did not have equal importance or value in her life. Early in her life, she resolved that her Christian faith was the foundation of her life, and everything else flowed directly from it. As much as she loved her family, friends, and the fight for freedom and equality, she never forgot that without her faith in Christ, nothing else mattered. In fact, it was precisely because of her unwavering faith that she was charged to love her *family, friends, and freedom*. And that is the hallmark of a well-ordered and well-lived life. Knowing what was most important in her life and arranging her priorities accordingly was a simple but successful life formula that guided her from childhood to her final breath. Those of us left here on this side can use that same formula, as we seek to live a well-ordered and well-lived life, as she so wonderfully did. Thank you, God, for allowing Daisy to show us how to live such a life.

Daisy was very pleased with my first book, *Gifts of Moments,* as it contained inspirational messages about faith, freedom, family, and friends. Because of her own devotion to those priorities and passions, the book's messages resonated strongly for her. She and I shared the belief that moments are gifts granted to us by God, and that those gifts come with a covenant to use them in the most beneficial manner possible—not exclusively for self, but primarily in the service to others. For those who knew her, they will attest to the fact that she spent her entire life in service to others. The second part of the book's title, Being Somebody to Somebody, also resonated very strongly for her. The idea that there is an obligation among all people, especially people of faith, to stop being *nobody to anybody* and start *being somebody to somebody*. Anyone who knew Daisy will state unequivocally that she spent her life being somebody to somebody.

It has been my pleasure to pen this tribute to her. Yet, even the words and pictures printed here do not fully capture the life and legacy of Daisy Harris Wade. For those of us who knew and loved her, memories are indelibly etched in our hearts and minds that can never be adequately expressed in words. A quote from Dr. King comes to mind when considering the limitations of words. *Occasionally, in life there are those moments of unutterable fulfillment which cannot be completely explained by those symbols we call words. Their meaning can only be articulated by the inaudible language of the heart.*

Writing about her was difficult at times and joyful at others. Memories flooded my heart and head that made me feel both joy and sorrow. There were two important things, however, that helped me to handle the sorrow. One, bathing myself in the memories of her warm, infectious smiles; genuine, hearty laughter; and sweet, reassuring voice; and two, listening to a recording of *Near the Cross* by Carlton Pearson. Sitting at my computer and hearing him sing, *til* my raptured soul finds rest beyond the river, I could not help but think about Daisy. I know that when she passed over, she found rest just beyond the river; and one day, all of us who love her, hope to see her again when we take our rest. *And as she would urge everyone to do right now, let's all say,* **"Amen!"**

RECIPES

Daisy's Famous Banana Pudding

2-3 ripe bananas, peeled and sliced

Bag of Jack's Vanilla Wafers (Daisy's preferred brand), although any brand will work.

Layer wafers and bananas in a baking dish and set aside.

Filling for pudding

3 medium size eggs. Separate the whites and the yolks. Set whites aside.

1. ½ cup of sugar

2. ½ tsp. of flour

3. 1 tsp. of vanilla flavoring

4. ½ stick of butter

5. ½ cup of evaporated milk (Daisy preferred Pet brand.)

6. ½ cup of water

7. Egg yolks

Mix items 1-7. Pour mixture into a pot. Stir while slowly bringing to a light boil.

Pour the mixture over the layers of bananas and vanilla wafers.

Beat or whisk the egg whites for meringue.

Spread the meringue evenly on top of the mixture and layers.

Place any remaining wafers around the edge of the baking dish.

Place baking dish in pre-heated oven at 350 degrees for about 10-15 minutes or until meringue browns.

Yellow Layer Cake with Buttery Frosting

Cake: ½ cup butter flavor shortening
1 and 1/3 cups of sugar
2 cups of all-purpose flour
1tsp of salt
3 tsps of baking powder
1 cup of milk
2 eggs

Preheat oven to 350 degrees
Combine sugar, flour, salt, and baking powder
Add butter flavor shortening and 2/3 cups of the milk and beat for 2 minutes at medium speed
Scrape bowl and beaters frequently
Add eggs and remainder of milk and mix for 2 minutes at medium speed
Pour half of batter into each of two 8-inch round pans
Bake at 350 degrees for 3-35 minutes

Frosting: ¼ cup of butter flavor shortening
3 cups of confectioners sugar
½ tsp of salt
1 and ½ tsps of Vanilla
¼ cup of milk

In medium mixing bowl combine 1 cup of sugar, butter flavor shortening, vanilla and salt. Add milk and remaining sugar, alternately blending until smooth and creamy.

Okra-Corn-Tomato

6 ears of corn

2 cups of cut up okra

¼ cup of margarine

2 teaspoon of margarine

3 medium tomatoes, chopped

1 tablespoon of sugar; Salt and pepper to taste.

Cut corn off each cob.

Cook and stir okra in ¼ cup of margarine in large skillet over medium

heat until tender, about 7 minutes

Add corn and 2 teaspoons of margarine

Cook uncovered until tender, 10-12 minutes

Stir in remaining ingredients. Cook for additional 10 minutes

Collard Greens and Corn on the Cob

Wash and shred several bunches of collard greens

Place in pot with a ham hock, water and mini ears of corn

Season to taste

Cook on medium heat for 35-45 minutes

Make sure corn is submerged in water to ensure doneness

When corn is tender, lower temperature and simmer for 15 minutes

String Beans and Potatoes

Drain and empty two cans of string beans into a pot of water. Do not cover beans entirely.
Add a few slices of bacon or salt meat

Peel and cube several white or red potatoes

Add potatoes to the pot of string beans

Stir in a can of tomato paste or sauce. Ketchup will also work.

Season to taste and boil until potatoes can be easily pierced with a fork.

About the Author

Anthony J. Harris was born in Hattiesburg, Mississippi. He was an active participant in the local Civil Rights Movement and has been a champion for ethical leadership for the greater part of his life. Dr. Harris has published a of scholarly articles and the following books: *Fruits of a Disgraced Legacy*, *It's What's on the Inside*, *Gifts of Moments: Being Somebody to Somebody*, and *Ain't Gonna Let Nobody Turn Me 'Round*. In his books, he draws upon life lessons learned through love, injustice, leadership, and power.

Dr. Harris has been featured on PBS and conducts keynote addresses on topics pertaining to the Civil Rights Movement, the Civil Rights

Movement, the educational success of young black males, and leadership. Since 2008, Dr. Harris has served as Professor of Education at Mercer University in Atlanta, Georgia. He and his wife, Smithenia, have two adult children, Ashley and Michael.

Connect Online: www.tandemlightpress.com/anthonyjharris.html

To arrange a speaking engagement with Anthony J. Harris, please contact the Tandem Light Press Speakers

Bureau at: speakersbureau@tandemlightpress.com.

www.ingramcontent.com/pod-product-compliance
Lightning Source LLC
Chambersburg PA
CBHW050558300426
44112CB00013B/1970

9780986166075